Essential Volunteer Management

2nd Edition

Steve McCurley
Rick Lynch

DIRECTORY OF SOCIAL CHANGE

Published by
The Directory of Social Change
24 Stephenson Way
London NW1 2DP
Tel: 0171 209 5151, fax: 0171 209 5049
e-mail: info@d-s-c.demon.co.uk
from whom further copies and a full publications list are available.

The Directory of Social Change is Registered Charity no. 800517

First published 1994
Revised Second Edition 1998

Cover photographs reproduced by kind permission of CSV (Community
Service Volunteers)/Alistair Berg and Simon Bannister.

ISBN 1 900360 18 7

British Library Cataloguing in Publication Data
A catalogue record for this book is available from the British Library

Cover design by Kate Bass
Designed and typeset by Kate Bass
Printed and bound by Page Bros., Norwich

Directory of Social Change London Office:
Courses and Conferences tel: 0171 209 4949
Charityfair tel: 0171 209 1015
Research tel: 0171 209 4422
Finance and Administration tel: 0171 209 0902

Directory of Social Change Northern Office:
3rd Floor, Federation House, Hope Street, Liverpool L1 9BW
Courses and Conferences tel: 0151 708 0117
Research tel: 0151 708 0136

The Directory of Social Change would like to thank the following
organisations for providing examples for this new edition:
The National Trust, The British Red Cross, REACH, and BTCV
(British Trust for Conservation Volunteers).

Contents

Foreword
By Alun Michael   5

Chapter One
An Introduction to Volunteer Management   7

Chapter Two
Volunteering Involement in your Mission   23

Chapter Three
Designing a Voluneer Programme   33

Chapter Four
Creating Motivating Volunteer Jobs   43

Chapter Five
Recruitment   57

Chapter Six
Screening and Interviewing   87

Chapter Seven
Orientation and Training   99

Chapter Eight
Supervision   111

Chapter Nine
Retention and Recognition   139

Chapter Ten
Volunteer-Staff Relations   161

Chapter Eleven
Some Final Suggestions   183

Appendix A
Sample policy on volunteer management   187

Appendix B
Sample forms to be used in
volunteer management   201

Further Reading   219

Useful Addresses   221

Foreword

As Minister with responsibility for the voluntary sector, community development and volunteering I am delighted to have been asked to write a few words for this revised edition of Rick Lynch and Steve McCurley's *Essential Volunteer Management.*

Volunteering is an essential element in citizenship and in re-establishing a sense of community. It is an activity which is valued very highly by this Government. Volunteers play an essential part in the diverse activities of the voluntary and public sectors. Voluntary activity is dynamic and innovative. It is pursued in large, national organisations, and in informal, local settings. Volunteers work in voluntary and statutory settings, in teams, and individually. This guide will be important to those who manage volunteers.

This guide will help the volunteer manager to plan effectively at all stages of the involvement of volunteers - including managing the recruitment process, keeping volunteers, supervising and supporting them, and demonstrating your appreciation of the contribution that they make. I wish such a valuable resource had been available to me when I needed it.

Volunteers make a tremendous contribution to society by giving freely of their time and talents, their energy and enthusiasm, and their experience. As well as supporting volunteering in all its forms, my aim is to ensure that volunteering is inclusive of all sections of society. Some people can feel excluded by the traditional volunteering structures and organisations. It is vital to ease the barriers to volunteering for those who currently feel excluded. For many, volunteering can help with their own personal development, to help them to build a sense of self worth, and to develop their talents. I hope that the good practice offered by this guide will assist organisations to make their volunteering opportunities accessible to all, and to provide a valuable experience.

I recommend this valuable guide to all those committed to or considering the involvement of volunteers.

ALUN MICHAEL
Minister of State, Home Office

CHAPTER ONE

An Introduction to Volunteer Management

ABOUT THIS BOOK

Essential Volunteer Management is an examination of the methods originally developed in the United States for operating a successful volunteer programme. It is designed to explain the approach that has made the American volunteer community one of the largest and most creative in the world. The publisher who has commissioned this book for the UK, feels that many of the techniques developed in the United States simply reflect a need to adjust the ways of involving and using volunteers to the changes that voluntary organisations and their members are experiencing – rapid growth in the number of organisations, increased complexity in personal lives, multi-diversity of population groups, and so on.

Topics covered include:

♦ **An overview of volunteering in both the UK and US**

♦ **Reasons for volunteering**

♦ **Changing styles of volunteers - and their implications**

♦ **Introduction to volunteer management and the role of the programme manager**

Since these factors are worldwide, it was felt that a review of the volunteer management approach in the United States might be of use to volunteer programme managers in the UK and other areas that are undergoing the same changes and stresses. However, where possible we have tried to include UK examples and case studies.

AN OVERVIEW OF VOLUNTEERING ACTIVITY

Volunteering in the United States

Volunteering has been a pervasive tradition throughout American history. Since the days of Alexis de Tocqueville, commentators have noted the American penchant for forming voluntary groups of citizens to work on mutual problems and interests.

Volunteering is one of the most common activities in American society with around 50% of the adult population involved at some level. In 1991 a US Gallup Poll revealed that almost 100 million adults had volunteered that year, contributing a total of over 20.5 billion hours of their time.

Volunteers come in all shapes, ages and sizes, and with almost half of the population engaged in volunteering, it should be no surprise that the typical volunteer can be almost anyone:

◆ volunteering stretches across all age categories, with the largest amount being done by those aged 30 to 45;

◆ volunteering is non-gender related, with equal involvement from males and females;

◆ the typical volunteer donated 4.2 hours per week to volunteering.

Overall distribution of volunteering by age category in the US is as follows:
   ◆ 48% of those 18-24
   ◆ 53% of those 25-34
   ◆ 61% of those 35-44
   ◆ 56% of those 45-54
   ◆ 49% of those 55-64
   ◆ 42% of those 65-74
   ◆ 27% of those 75+

Volunteering is also pervasive by employment category:
   ◆ 67% of those full-time self employed
   ◆ 59% of those part-time self employed
   ◆ 62% of those part-time employed by someone else
   ◆ 57% of those full-time employed by someone else
   ◆ 43% of those not employed

The recipients of volunteer time are equally varied. Most of the time was given by those engaged in formal volunteer work for organisations. About 70% of that went to *non-profit organisations*; 20% went to *government organisations*; and 10% went to *for-profit organisations* (mostly hospitals and nursing homes).

The importance of volunteers to these organisations can scarcely be over-stated. For non-profit organisations, volunteers can often make the difference between remaining in operation or being forced to close. In some ways volunteers are as important to charitable causes as are donations of money – in the US in 1991, the estimated value of volunteer services was *$176 billion* and represented the equivalent of *9 million full-time employees*.

Volunteering in the United Kingdom

Volunteering is now gaining a higher profile in the UK with more people becoming aware of the opportunities available. The economic recession of the late 1980s also heightened interest; voluntary organisations are now looking to increase volunteer involvement, and volunteering is very much on the political agenda. In 1992 the main political parties renewed their commitment to encourage volunteering. In March 1994, the Government's 'Make a Difference' programme was launched to increase individual involvement in the community, and the UK's first ever Volunteering Strategy was launched in June 1995.

In 1997 the Labour Government launched its New Deal for the unemployed. Participation will be compulsory for all job-seekers aged 18 to 24 who have been unemployed for more than 6 months, and for over 25-year-olds who have been unemployed for more than 2 years. It aims to improve the employability of young people by offering them several options for work experience. This includes a Voluntary Sector option which aims to increase and improve the benefits and services to local communities provided by voluntary and community groups. Within this option for example, an Environment Task Force has been set up, and those involved will be encouraged to contribute to the regeneration and conservation of the environment and local communities.

Participants will be expected to work a minimum of 30 hours a week over five days and to conduct a structured job search. They will be paid an amount equivalent to the Job Seekers Allowance, together with a grant of £400 per month in weekly or fortnightly payments. Placements must be of high quality and offer training and practical experience in the essential skills and behaviour sought by employers. Participants will also receive support and advice in their search for permanent work.

In October 1997 the Government also launched Millennium Volunteers, a scheme to provide volunteering opportunities for young people. It will be kick-started by £15 million from the windfall levy (a tax levied on the profits of the privatised utilities). Young people aged 16 to 24 will be able to volunteer for a wide range of activities which will not only help the community, but will enable them to develop skills and improve their employment prospects.

The fact that volunteering appears to be on the increase will be seen as encouraging by those who support an expanded role for the voluntary sector and a more pluralist approach to welfare provision. The challenge is now to harness this growth to play a supportive, supplementary role both to statutory services and the wider community.

Reasons for volunteering

Volunteers get involved for a variety of reasons. The most often cited are:

- *"I wanted to help others."*
- *"I felt obligated to give back what I got."*
- *"A sense of civic duty."*
- *"Religious convictions."*
- *"I wanted to make a difference in the world."*
- *"I believe in the cause."*

These altruistic reasons are accompanied by self-interest motivations:

- *"I wanted to gain work experience and learn new skills."*
- *"I like meeting new friends and being involved."*
- *"I felt I could impress my employer and show leadership."*
- *"It made me feel needed."*
- *"It allowed me to experience new lifestyles and cultures."*
- *"I do it because my job is boring and this lets me have fun."*

Many volunteers get involved for reasons having to do with their families:

- *"It's a good way to spend time with my family."*
- *"I wanted to set an example for my children."*
- *"I had to get involved so that my children would have the benefit of the programme."*
- *"I wanted to give back some of the help that members of my family have received."*

The opportunities for working with volunteers have never been more promising. A typical volunteer will experience a variety of motivations, ranging from the purely altruistic to the highly self-interested, although these motivations may change during their volunteering career. They will also see their motivation vary considerably from organisation to organisation and even over time within a single organisation.

The pattern of a volunteer's connection with an organisation or cause will also vary. The typical volunteer in the US is involved with two organisations at any one time, although these tend to change over the years. Some volunteers prefer to work with many organisations, changing from group to group within the course of a single year. Others are committed to a specific cause, remaining with that group for years or even decades and contributing hundreds of hours of time.

A well-run volunteer programme attempts to develop opportunities for both these styles of involvement.

CHANGING STYLES OF VOLUNTEER INVOLVEMENT

Volunteering is going through several changes related to the way in which people choose to participate. We seem to be moving toward a system in which there are two distinct types of volunteers.

The long-term volunteer

The long-term volunteer matches the common notion of the person who is dedicated to a cause or a group. Given below are the main characteristics of the long-term volunteer.

◆ *Dedication to a cause or an organisation.* The long-term volunteer has a strong sense of affiliation with the organisation and its volunteer effort. They consider themselves to be owners of the effort. Long-term volunteers often have a strong emotional investment in their volunteer role and in the sense of personal worth and identity they gain from their participation.

◆ The long-term volunteer is commonly recruited in one of three ways. By *self-recruitment* (finding the organisation on their own because of an existing personal commitment to the cause), by *growth from within* (becoming increasingly connected over time), or by *cloning*, that is, being brought to the organisation because of a close connection to the existing circle of volunteers.

◆ The long-term volunteer will tend to shape their own job, adapting their time and energies to whatever is necessary to make the cause succeed. Long-term volunteers tend to be generalists, willing to do whatever type of work is required to make the effort function, although this may not be exciting or rewarding in itself.

◆ Motivation for the long-term volunteer is a matter of both achievement and affiliation, and often recognition is best expressed as an opportunity for greater involvement or advancement in the cause or the organisation.

Many established organisations have relied for years on long-term volunteers, designing jobs that require a steady donation of time over a prolonged period. In many cases these long-term volunteers were the actual creators of the organisation from whom they continued volunteering, helping found a structure which they later joined.

The primary supply for this type of volunteer has traditionally been middle and upper income housewives, who have the free time to donate, are able to offer steady hours and who have often used volunteering to give meaning and significance to their lives, making it their equivalent of a successful career.

Of course, long-term volunteers are not drawn solely from this category, and there are many unemployed, retired and lower income volunteers who contribute their time on a long-term basis.

The short-term volunteer

Over the last ten years, a different style of volunteering has begun to develop. For purposes of comparison, this style might be called that of the *short-term volunteer*. Given below are the main characteristics of the short-term volunteer.

♦ A general interest in an organisation or cause, but not necessarily one of extreme depth. Whilst they support the cause, they do not usually view the organisation or their involvement as a central part of their own life.

♦ The short-term volunteer is usually actively recruited to join the organisation. This can happen in one of three ways.

1. They connect with an organisation because of a particular volunteer job in which they are interested. It is the type of work that attracts them, not necessarily what the organisation is trying to accomplish.

2. They are recruited through participation in a specific event, such as a weekend sports programme or race. It will usually be the type of event that attracts them, or the social activity which it allows, and not the organisation or cause.

3. They are recruited by forced choice, that is they are asked by a friend or employer to volunteer. Commonly they volunteer because of their personal connection with the requester, not from any knowledge of or commitment to the organisation or cause.

◆ Short-term volunteers want a well-defined job of limited duration. They want to know at the beginning of their volunteering exactly what they are being asked to do and for how long they are committed to do it. Many short-term volunteers can be considered specialists, because they are only with the organisation long enough to learn one job or are only willing to perform one kind of work. Usually the more limited the expected time commitment and the better delineated the scope of work, the easier it will be to recruit the short-term volunteer. A short-term volunteer may well volunteer throughout their life, but they do not usually remain too long with any one organisation, or they will only work on tasks which allow them to closely control the amount of time they donate.

◆ Motivating the short-term volunteer is a matter of recognising their personal achievement, not their status within the group. It is a matter of thanking them for their contribution and allowing them to move on.

Oddly enough, an individual may be a short-term volunteer with one group and a long-term volunteer with another group.

On balance, it seems there is a clear shift toward a preference for short-term volunteering. In attempting to cope with competing demands from work, home, leisure activities, and so on, potential volunteers are choosing to limit their participation by changing the way in which they become involved.

New types of volunteers

As a result, voluntary organisations find themselves confronted by totally new types of volunteers.

Employer supported volunteers

The UK is seeing a steady increase in employer supported volunteering. The National Centre For Volunteering began work in employer supported volunteering in the early 1980s with the Ashridge employee volunteering conference and the Crossover Project, which encouraged volunteering in the years immediately prior to retirement. In 1990 Whitbread organised a national conference for companies and published a *Guide to Employee Volunteering*.

In 1990 Business In The Community (BITC) began a two year campaign to promote employer supported volunteering as one of a number of forms of corporate community involvement. In addition, the Action Resource Centre (ARC), which was set up to promote secondment, also became interested in employees volunteering. In 1993 ARC was merged with the Employee Volunteering Campaign at BITC to form a new unit known as Action: Employees in The Community. The National Centre For Volunteering continues to offer a range of products and services for community organisations and employees interested in developing employer supported volunteering programmes.

Practice varies, but the typical employee volunteer will participate with a small group of colleagues for a few hours a month doing something quite practical. Those employees with particular professional or technical skills may also be encouraged to offer those skills where they are needed, and senior managers may even be encouraged to serve as trustees or management committee members. NatWest Bank, for example, had 1,200 of its staff serving as trustees in the early 1990s.

In larger companies there may be an Employee Volunteer Coordinator responsible for encouraging volunteering, finding volunteering opportunities and offering support to employee volunteers. Some large companies offer cash awards, typically £100 or £500, to those organisations that their employees volunteer with. There is now an annual competition for the best company volunteering programme.

Older volunteers

The experience and commitment of the senior community has begun to be tapped in earnest. Many retired business people are recruited to assist in the management of voluntary organisations. The American Association of Retired Persons has created a nationwide Volunteer Talent Bank to assist groups in making use of the volunteer skills of its membership.

In the UK, the Retired Action Clearing House (REACH) and Community Service Volunteers' Retired and Senior Volunteering Programme (RSVP) both encourage retired volunteering and place volunteers in suitable jobs.

The demographics of society and work show an increasing elderly population, as people live longer and many people retire or are being retired before the statutory retirement age. This means there will be a larger pool of active retirees to draw upon as volunteers, and to deal with the increasing need to provide services to older people as the statutory social and health services become more stretched.

This presents new challenges and new opportunities. Retirees can be recruited to an unpaid or expenses-only second career, attracted into traditional volunteering opportunities, or volunteer in completely new ways — such as the University of the Third Age (U3A) where retired people run courses or classes for retired people.

Alternative sentencing volunteers

In recent years the US has seen a tremendous growth in the use of 'volunteering' as a form of sentencing following a conviction for criminal behaviour. Indeed, mandatory sentencing to community service hours is now a regular part of sentencing for plea bargained agreements.

A broadly similar form of rehabilitative sentencing in the UK is the Community Service Order. However, because of the compulsory component of activities undertaken through these orders, CSO activity is not considered 'volunteering' as defined by The National Centre For Volunteering or Make a Difference.

There are also intermediate treatment schemes for young people at risk of offending and for young offenders. Some of these involve community service. Two national organisations promote such schemes – the National Association for the Care and Resettlement of Offenders (NACRO) and Community Service Volunteers (CSV).

Professional volunteers

Many associations of professionals have developed active programmes to encourage, and in some cases require, members of their profession to perform community work. The accounting and legal professions have been instrumental in creating a culture of community involvement within their ranks. Some of this volunteering consists of performing the work of their profession on behalf of community groups or individuals.

The Institute of Chartered Accountants, the Law Society, the Society of Industrial Artists and Designers, and the Royal Institute of Chartered Surveyors, for example, all encourage members to give their free time and become actively involved.

One interesting initiative in the UK is Lawyers in the Community, a scheme run by Action: Employees in the Community to encourage lawyers to serve as trustees and committee members.

Episodic volunteers

These are volunteers who go from organisation to organisation, getting involved in one-off events, then move on to other events at other organisations. They may participate with an organisation on an annual basis, contributing to running an event each year, but limiting their participation to that event. In the US there are formal groups of such volunteers, such as City Cares, who have targeted young adults as participants in these group volunteer activities. In many ways, these groups are taking the place of the social clubs which have traditionally provided volunteers for many years.

Transitional volunteers

Individuals who are changing lifestyles (housewives re-entering the job market, those with emotional disturbances moving back into interaction with others, those with disabilities learning new skills, etc.) have often undertaken volunteering as an activity to forge a path back into the community.

Often this transitional volunteering takes place informally, with people recognising that volunteering might be the next step for them. One interesting scheme is Working for a Charity, which provides a twenty-day volunteer assignment plus seven days of training over a three-month period for those looking for a return to work or a career change.

Unemployed volunteers

Unemployed people often begin volunteering as a way of developing skills which may lead to paid employment. In some areas of the US, volunteering is a *requirement* for those who are receiving government benefits while unemployed.

This approach is now also being tried in the UK. Volunteering offers an alternative opportunity for involvement when work is not available, but attracting this group and making their involvement a success, not least for them, requires new thinking and new approaches. Amongst the unemployed are many who are low-skilled and who have become completely unused to work and working relationships.

There have been a succession of government programmes to involve the long-term unemployed in meaningful community work. The most recent government scheme - the New deal, or 'Welfare to work' programme is discussed more fully on p9.

Organisations such as CITE (Associates) Ltd and Charity Action have become agents for recruiting and placing unemployed people on assignments lasting from six months to one year.

Stipended volunteers

Even those who receive a small payment for their services have become part of the volunteer community. Several programmes in the US (such as the Senior Companion Program or the Foster Grandparents Program) pay small stipends to volunteers. The National Service volunteer programme enacted in the US aimed to recruit 100,000 volunteers in the first three years, with each volunteer receiving both a small living allowance and a college-tuition benefit.

In the UK, recent legal developments suggest the need to define the difference between volunteers and paid workers. If a volunteer is paid for their services (with the exception of reasonable expenses, for travel, for example), there may be tax implications for the organisation.

Few of these types of volunteer workers would have been recognised twenty years ago, and many are still startling to organisations who have not worked with them before. Recognising their different motivations and particular needs is important. Yet each simply represents a new way to enable individuals from the community to be of service to others.

THE IMPLICATIONS OF CHANGING STYLES & TYPES OF VOLUNTEER

These changes in the types of volunteer have impacted volunteer management in several ways.

◆ They have necessitated major changes in job design and recruitment techniques. Some organisations seeking volunteers have been forced to make jobs smaller and more manageable and to cater more to the requirements of the volunteer, such as availability and duration. It is worth bearing in mind that with proper training and support, volunteers can be developed to undertake more challenging opportunities. Similarly, highly skilled volunteers may want volunteering opportunities which are not particularly taxing.

◆ Some organisations have encountered difficulties in adjusting to new types of volunteers, particularly when several types have been mixed together. As an example, long-term volunteers may well view short-term volunteers as uncaring or uncommitted to the organisation. The lack of willingness of the short-term volunteer to sacrifice their own life to the interests of the cause can be misunderstood or even resented by the long-term volunteer. Difficulties with different types of volunteers can be overcome through a number of strategies, including planning and consultation with staff and existing volunteers.

◆ To get enough long-term volunteers – who are actually more desirable, easier to manage and highly necessary for some leadership volunteer functions – organisations are having to rely more on promotion from within, grooming volunteers to assume more responsibilities and slowly convincing them to commit more time. Much more effort has to be invested in each volunteer to develop them to their potential.

◆ Organisations are facing greater competition for all types of volunteer. Increasingly, the volunteer is in a favourable bargaining position, sought by several organisations, and able to choose the situation which best meets their own needs and interests.

Styles of volunteer management

Volunteer programmes also vary in style of operation and management. One might picture a range of programmes, from those that are very structured, with a high degree of permanent staff supervision of volunteers (such as a volunteer programme to aid those who are in prison), to those that are operated primarily by volunteers themselves (such as a Neighbourhood Watch programme).

While the principles of volunteer management remain the same in both styles of programme, the exact methods used will vary from the more institutional to the more personal. The operational style of the volunteer programme has to fit the culture of the organisation.

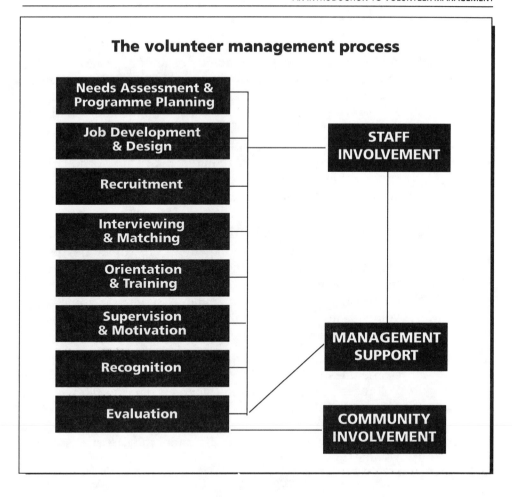

The volunteer management process

Effective volunteer management requires a planned and organised process similar to that required by any organisational project or effort.

The descending steps on the left side of the diagram *(above)* represent the major elements involved in determining the needs for volunteers within the organisation, identifying suitable volunteers, and then creating a motivational structure which will support those volunteers. They are roughly analogous to the personnel and supervisory procedures for paid staff. The elements on the right side of the figure represent the other universes which interact with and must support volunteer personnel (the community at large, upper management of the organisation, and staff with whom volunteers will be in contact) and which therefore must be involved in the process of volunteer management.

All of these elements are interactive and, as in most creative management processes, rarely proceed in a linear fashion. During the existence of the overall volunteer programme, elements within this process will tend to recur with the addition of each new area of volunteer use (as new projects are created for example), and with the addition of each new volunteer (as the process is customised to the requirements of the individual). The process will also be re-enacted as new staff who interact with volunteers are taken on.

The role of the volunteer programme manager

The roles of volunteer management are sometimes played haphazardly by individual members of staff. Organisations which involve volunteers most effectively, however, do so as part of a coordinated volunteer programme. A systematic approach to volunteer involvement requires someone to plan and coordinate all the activities of the volunteer management process.

This does not mean that the Volunteer Programme Manager (sometimes called the Volunteer Coordinator or Director of Volunteers) supervises all the volunteers directly, although they may in a small organisation where volunteers work in a stand alone programme. If all the volunteers work in a thrift shop, for example, they may work directly under the supervision of the Volunteer Coordinator.

Many volunteer programmes start out this way. As volunteers start to become involved in other aspects of the organisation, however, the Volunteer Coordinator quickly reaches the limits of this ability to supervise volunteers directly. At this point, volunteers start to work under the direct supervision of other paid staff. An accounting student, for example, might volunteer in the administrative office, supervised by the chief accountant.

The effective volunteer plays a critical role in the success of the entire organisation. When new projects or new directions arise, the role of volunteers is planned into them from the beginning. The Volunteer Coordinator helps top management identify necessary expertise that will help the project succeed, and works with paid staff to design volunteer jobs to meet those needs. They plan and coordinate a recruitment effort to find people who will find such work fulfilling enough to devote their leisure time to doing it, assist in the screening, interviewing, and selection processes, provide an overall orientation to the organisation, evaluate the success of the volunteer programme and plan recognition events.

The major role of the modern Volunteer Programme Manager is thus not working directly with volunteers, save those they recruit to help them in these processes. Rather they focus attention on paid staff, securing top management support for volunteer efforts and helping individual staff do a good job of managing and retaining their volunteer helpers.

Not-for-profit organisations that excel in serving their clients realise they can never hire enough paid expertise to achieve their missions fully. To succeed, they must therefore encourage concerned people to donate their expertise just as they encourage people to provide financial support. In this, staff should value the Volunteer Programme Manager as much as they do the (usually much higher paid) fundraiser. The importance of volunteering in relation to fundraising is clear for those organisations where the value of the volunteer time is far in excess of the cash they raise and spend each year. The lack of importance given to volunteering is shown by the often unfulfilled potential of this resource, whether it is being used directly to further the organisation's work or just to raise money for it.

Unfortunately, in too many organisations, the volunteer programme is regarded as an optional extra to benefit those with time on their hands. The role of the Volunteer Coordinator is undervalued in such organisations, and volunteers are largely confined to menial or clerical functions that are not directly related to the organisation's mission. Such organisations are overwhelmed by the problems they exist to solve, spending more and more resources chasing elusive grants and donations.

Effective organisations in the 1990s are involving volunteers in ever more significant roles. Volunteers, drawn from all walks of life and with all manner of skills, will be involved as equal partners with staff in pursuing the organisation's goals. When staff plan new efforts, they will identify needs for expertise and plan to involve volunteers to meet them. In order to accomplish this, top management must give more status, support, and resources to the Volunteer Programme Manager.

We will be working with three simple shapes:

The Square
Representing the process of developing jobs within the organisation.

The Circles
Representing the individual needs of the volunteer and the collective needs of the organisation.

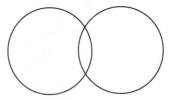

The Triangle
Representing the network of relationships among the volunteers, the Volunteer Manager and the organisation staff.

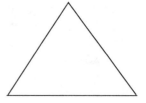

Taken together, these three shapes illustrate the major tasks which must be accomplished in order for volunteer management to be effective.

The geometry of volunteer involvement

Another way of looking at the process of volunteer management can be represented through the use of simple geometric figures (*above*). These geometric figures illustrate how interacting processes of volunteer management work. Throughout this book we will be referring to these figures as a way of demonstrating what ought to be happening in the process of managing a volunteer programme.

CHAPTER TWO

Volunteer Involvement in Your Mission

CREATING A MISSION

An effective volunteer programme begins with the mission of the organisation. The mission is a statement of the purpose of the organisation and its ultimate goal. When this goal is achieved, the organisation will no longer need to exist. Whatever role volunteers have within an organisation they will be expected to work towards the achievement of this overall aim. Any statement about a volunteer's particular role should

Topics covered include:

◆ **Creating a mission statement**

◆ **Developing a vision for your organisation**

◆ **Defining the role of volunteers**

therefore fit within the overall mission. A literacy programme, for example, might have as its mission 'putting an end to functional illiteracy in the community', and volunteers might be asked to provide tutoring services to functionally illiterate adults. A statement such as 'We exist to provide hot meals to senior citizens' is not an effective mission statement. One that says 'Our mission is to put an end to senior malnutrition' is.

In the US, an exhaustive study of sixteen organisations in four cities conducted by the Points of Light Foundation, found that one of the hallmarks of an effective volunteer programme is the way in which the mission is defined. If the volunteer programme is to be a means of solving a community problem or meeting a community need, the mission of the organisation must be phrased in terms of that problem. Thus the first step in planning an effective volunteer programme is to define the mission of the organisation in such terms.

In the case of non-profit organisations involved in direct service activities, the mission will be to address the need of the clients they serve. Mission statements that define what the organisation does on a daily basis do not galvanize followers as readily as mission statements that talk about meeting a need or solving a problem. It may sound tedious or boring to prepare and serve hot meals, but it is rewarding to help put an end to senior

Sample Mission Statements

Youth organisation

"Many young people grow up without the skills and self-confidence to become competent, successful adults. Our mission is to equip youth to have a fulfilling, successful life, however they may define it."

Mental Health Centre

"Many people are in doubt, fear, and pain in our community. Our mission is to help them cope with this condition so as to prevent their doing harm to themselves and others and to help them return to independent living as productive members of the community."

Community Action Agency

"Our mission is to help people overcome their poverty and become self-sufficient."

Volunteer Centre

"Many people in our community are concerned about community problems but either feel powerless to do anything about them or don't know how to get involved in the solution. At the same time, many agencies in our community are unable to meet fully the needs of their clients due to lack of personpower. Our mission is to solve both of these problems by providing an avenue for people to get involved in meaningful volunteer work."

malnutrition. Missions that describe what a group does also tend to limit the organisation to that activity and to lock people into doing things because they 'have always done it that way'. They tend to promote the status quo and so make effective change impossible.

Who should develop the mission statement?

The mission statement is usually written when an organisation is formed, in order to clarify its aims and the need it was established to address. It should be developed with the involvement of the people who will be carrying out the mission. This ensures that they feel a sense of ownership in the mission. The leader should facilitate this process by asking questions such as "What is our purpose? What is the need in the outside world that we are trying to meet? Under what circumstances could we happily go out of business?"

Often a group will assume that such a discussion will take only a few minutes. The mission seems obvious to each person. However, they are invariably surprised to discover that there are small or even major differences of opinion. Many mission-setting meetings turn out to be gruelling, frustrating events that last for hours or even days. The effort is worth it, however, because it enables each person to connect their actions to the ultimate purpose of the organisation. It thus creates meaning in the lives of people, a fundamental component of motivation and dedication.

Sometimes a discussion of the mission will uncover a deep conflict between some segments of the group. Where the mission is assumed rather than explicit, these conflicts tend to play themselves out in petty politics, their roots obscured by the issues of the day. At an art museum, for example, the discussion of the mission uncovered a conflict between most of the curators, who thought that the mission was to preserve valuable works of art, and others who thought the mission should be to provide the public with the works of art they wanted to see. Others were adamant that the purpose of the museum was to expand the taste of the public for all forms of art. Until this discussion, there had been many conflicts about the types of exhibitions and programmes the museum should sponsor, conflicts that had turned into nasty, personal in-fighting. As the group discussed the mission, they suddenly understood the source of the conflict and came to understand each other's behaviour.

The mission statement should not be some dusty paragraph that is locked away in a drawer, liberated only to preface grant proposals. It should be a statement that galvanizes the volunteers and staff, a statement from which their daily activities draw meaning. It should be a living declaration of what the group is trying to accomplish. It should be a statement of the difference the group intends to make in the world.

Developing a strategy to achieve the mission

The mission statement is also the foundation of strategic planning. This involves three basic steps:

1. identifying obstacles to accomplishing the mission;
2. developing a strategy to overcome each obstacle;
3. setting goals to implement the strategy.

An example of this process comes from an agency whose mission is to solve the problem of teen drug abuse in a large city. Paid staff and volunteers identified peer pressure at school as one of several major obstacles to accomplishing this mission. This obstacle was a particular problem when youths left treatment programmes and returned to their high schools because their peer group encouraged them to return to their old ways. The strategy they chose to overcome that obstacle was to create an environment where youths who had been through treatment would experience positive peer pressure. This led to the decision to set a strategic goal of overcoming that obstacle by starting an alternative high school for recovering, chemically dependent teens.

An effective plan should also take into consideration the resources outside the group that could help to meet the need. An additional strategic object could be to mobilise those resources outside the group's normal environment as a new means of resolving any obstacles that impede its work. In the above case, for example, the group identified the city's major newspapers as an external resource which had not previously been identified as a means of overcoming any of their obstacles. The group asked what purpose the newspapers could serve in achieving their mission of overcoming teen drug abuse. It decided that, whilst the papers were highlighting the negative consequences of drug abuse, they were failing to let teenagers know about the successes former drug users were making of their lives. The group thus developed a new goal of persuading the newspapers to help them achieve their mission by giving greater coverage to these success stories.

Having created a strategy for achieving the mission, most non-profit organisations find that they lack the financial resources to hire enough people to accomplish all their goals. The common reaction to this is to prioritise those goals and pursue only the most important. A more effective approach is to look at how volunteers could help accomplish the mission of the organisation.

It is at this point that the volunteer programme becomes a critical and integral part of the organisation's success. Instead of being limited to pursuing a few objectives, the organisation can pursue all its objectives with total commitment. However, developing a volunteer programme often involves creating a new vision of the role of volunteers in the organisation as a whole.

CREATING A VISION STATEMENT

Sometimes people get mission and vision confused. The mission statement should be a one paragraph or one sentence statement of the organisation's purpose. It is a statement of why the group exists. The vision is a more detailed description of what the organisation intends to do to achieve its mission, and a statement of the role of volunteers should therefore be an integral part of it.

A good vision statement should be mission focused, and it should include the broad elements of the strategic plan. Creating an effective vision involves answering the following questions:

◆ who do we need to influence in order to accomplish our mission?
◆ what do we want them to do?

A systematic way to do this is to list the obstacles the group faces in accomplishing its mission and the resources (both actual and potential) that could help in moving toward the mission. The groups and individuals that show up on this list are people the organisation should try to influence.

As an example, the board and staff of a history museum identified the following interest groups:

◆ regional government officials (county)
◆ the local newspaper
◆ tourists
◆ people who use the museum for research
◆ the Chamber of Commerce
◆ local government officials (city)
◆ local businesses
◆ a local developer
◆ local schools.

After identifying such groups, the next task is to ask "What do we want these people to do for us?" In the case of the museum, the answers were as follows:

Regional Government:
✔ give us regular funding
✔ give us a one-off grant to help us purchase a new building

The Local Newspaper:
✔ give coverage of museum events
✔ highlight our value to the community

Researchers:
✔ write letters of support to funding sources
✔ donate materials to enhance our collection

Tourists:
✔ visit the museum (and pay admission fees)
✔ spread a positive impression of the museum
✔ buy things at the gift shop
✔ buy food in the restaurant

The Chamber of Commerce:
✔ provide information to members about museum events
✔ encourage members to support the museum financially

Local Government:
✔ provide regular funding

Local Businesses:
✔ contribute to the fund for a new building
✔ donate gifts in kind, such as chairs and desks

A Local Developer:
✔ donate a plot of land on which a new museum building can be built

The Schools:
✔ make our educational offerings part of the curriculum
✔ give students credit for volunteering at the museum
✔ support our funding requests

These answers create a sense of an ideal position for the organisation and a powerful vision of what the organisation should strive towards. A vision statement of the ideal future for this museum might read as follows:

In the year 2000, the XYZ History Museum moved into a new building, a replica of a nineteenth-century hotel that was destroyed by fire in 1928. The site was donated by a local developer and features a view of the harbour. The building was partly funded by private donations and partly by a grant from local government. Funding for four staff is secure through an endowment fund and the regular budget contributions of local government and the public schools. In addition, grants have been received from regional government sources for special projects and exhibits. The chamber of commerce is active in helping the museum acquire new objects of historical interest. Each year, students compete for the fifteen volunteer slots where they serve in a variety of exciting capacities.

The new museum building is a popular tourist attraction, with people coming to see the exhibits, buy gifts, and relax at the cafe. Local residents are able to show off the museum to their visitors. Scholars travel from across the region to work in the new research room. Their letters of thanks have helped to secure funding for future special projects. The high school uses museum resources to assist in teaching local history. The museum is such a popular attraction, that it has encouraged several local businesses to set up nearby, increasing the vitality of the neighbourhood.

Such a statement sets an ambitious and stretching set of goals for the new museum. At first, these may seem daunting, but as volunteers and paid staff make small steps toward the realisation of the vision, the sense of purpose and excitement grows. They begin to picture the type of institution they are creating, and that picture gives meaning to their daily actions.

Another way to formulate a vision is for a group to address the following question:

If we were going to go across the street and start a rival organisation, what would we do to make our present organisation obsolete?

This question helps people escape the bonds of what is, so they can think about what ought to be. It therefore helps the organisation escape the trap of its own past so it can renew itself. The aim is to identify what makes your organisation unique.

In the case of the history museum, such an exercise led them to add this paragraph to their vision statement:

"The museum attracts top staff because of its training programme, location, and public support. Staff and volunteer workspaces are furnished with a combination of modern equipment and antique furniture. Volunteers who started in high school often continue their volunteer work as adults. A self-supporting, on-site, child care service is free for staff and volunteers and also serves the community. An atmosphere of mutual support and camaraderie exists among staff and volunteers."

To give another example, a community organisation whose mission was to meet the recreational needs of the community considered what they would do if they were to start a competing organisation across the street. They wanted to create an organisation that would be more appealing to users and volunteers than their present organisation. The following is a list of some of their ideas:

◆ offer twenty-four hour child care
◆ offer evening aerobics classes
◆ have large and small rooms for community activities
◆ own a bus to take residents to the hall
◆ have fashion shows
◆ have an island kitchen with microwave ovens
◆ have a well-trained executive board skilled in volunteer management
◆ encourage a neighbourhood pub to open next door
◆ sponsor neighbourhood picnics and parties
◆ begin an adopt-a-neighbour programme
◆ have plush carpets
◆ have a pool table and table-tennis facilities
◆ have a carpentry shop that could be rented out to community residents
◆ have board meetings in luxurious locations
◆ have toys and games for kids
◆ have a good sound system
◆ hold dances and discos
◆ install skateboard ramps
◆ operate a sports equipment store at the hall.

This process gave them the ideas to develop a vision statement of where they wanted the organisation to go, and what they wanted to achieve.

Creating a vision of volunteer involvement

After an organisation comes up with a vision statement, some group members might say "but we could never do that. It would take too much money. It isn't realistic." The truth of the matter is, that with enough desire, you can do anything you wish. If you don't imagine a better situation, you are unlikely to get one. If you can be stopped by a thought in your heads, what will you do when you encounter a real obstacle?

More importantly, this negative sentiment ignores the major impact that using volunteers could have to the realisation of the vision. If an organisation believes "we could never do that," it is usually only focusing on its own limited resources. It needs to think bigger. It needs to realise that a volunteer programme will provide access to the wider resources of the community.

The Points of Light Foundation found that in organisations where volunteers were most effective there was a widely understood, well articulated vision of the role of volunteers. This vision should be an integral part of the overall vision of the organisation.

A vision for volunteer involvement gives a sense of the future the organisation is trying to create and the part volunteers will play in creating it. It also produces a sense of excitement and achievement among the volunteers by giving them a commonality of purpose. Part of the vision should be internal, showing what the organisation will look like, how it will operate and how volunteers will fit in to the overall picture. Part of it should focus on the organisation's strategic goals and should provide a positive role for volunteers to play in mission-critical activities.

The 'Changing the Paradigm' project of the Points of Light Foundation suggests some aspects of that vision:

◆ staff and volunteers work together as equals;

◆ staff are empowered to identify and create any volunteer job;

◆ the organisation learns from the experience of volunteers;

◆ there is a recognition of the value of volunteers in mission-critical activities;

- there is a central point for volunteer management in the agency;
- all staff play a role in developing jobs for and supervising volunteers.

Summary

The volunteer programme should not be seen as an add-on to the essential work of the organisation, but as an integral part of its efforts to achieve its mission. An effective volunteer programme gives an agency access to all the skills in the community. The vision for the volunteer programme both guides the efforts of those involved and encourages them to contribute their utmost to help achieve the organisation's overall objectives. As the director of a volunteer programme, you will be responsible for helping to develop that vision.

"An effective volunteer programme gives you access to all the skills in the community."

CHAPTER THREE
Designing a Volunteer Programme

As outlined in chapter two, an effective volunteer programme is one that makes a significant contribution to achieving the organisation's mission. In planning the volunteer programme, the director of volunteers should begin with this concept.

When organisations plan their work, they usually allow themselves to be constrained by the extent of their financial resources. They plan to do only what they can within the limits of the staff they can afford to hire and the things they can afford to buy. An effective volunteer programme frees organisations from some of these constraints and provides all the resources of the community necessary to help the agency accomplish its mission.

Non-profit organisations exist to solve problems or meet needs in communities. These problems are usually far greater in magnitude than the resources of the organisation. Very often the only way they will ever make a serious difference in their communities is through the involvement of volunteers who work on the problem in a variety ways. When volunteers are involved in this way, staff come to regard the volunteer programme as one which gives them access to all the skills they need to make a difference. The volunteer manager becomes the one who has "the keys to the kingdom".

Topics covered include:

- **Planning a volunteer programme**
- **Who should design the programme**
- **Getting staff involved**
- **Assessing your plan**

THE IMPORTANCE OF PLANNING

Some volunteer efforts have suffered from the problems generated by 'spontaneous creation'. This occurs when an over-enthusiastic administrator learns of the potential of volunteer involvement and pronounces at a staff meeting: *"Let there be volunteers!"*.

The assumption is that instituting a volunteer effort is simple and can be done instantly. The pronouncement is usually followed by the designation of an unsuspecting staff person as 'in charge of volunteers', with the immediate assignment of 'going out and rounding up a bunch of them'.

This simple-minded approach might work if all that is required is bringing in a few volunteers specifically to work on a single project, with no expectation that they will stay beyond that project or attempt to work on other activities. The approach will not work at all when considered on an institutional basis, where volunteers and staff are expected to work together on an on-going basis on a variety of programmes and tasks throughout the organisation.

Effective volunteer management is simple in theory, but subtle in operation. It has all the complexities of basic personnel management – job development, interviewing, supervision, evaluation of performance, recognition and reward. It also has complexities all of its own. An interesting example, not seen as often in the environment of paid staff, is that of the over-enthusiastic worker. Quite often, a volunteer manager will have to deal with a volunteer who causes difficulties for the project, not from a lack of motivation, but from a surplus of it. This volunteer will be so dedicated to the cause that they will expect and work for instant solutions to any problem that arises, and will not understand why the system sometimes operates so slowly. The volunteer may become impatient and infuriated with anyone, paid staff or volunteers, who doesn't give total dedication to making the system work perfectly, and immediately.

Effective volunteer programmes do not happen spontaneously, and they do not happen by accident. A well-designed programme is the result of good planning, and many decisions need to be made before any volunteers are sought.

Fitting together the puzzle

In a way, one might think about volunteer management within an organisation as the construction of a puzzle (see diagram on right).

Over recent years, the configurations of this puzzle have become increasingly complicated. The size of the square has increased, as organisations have developed broader uses for volunteers, involving volunteers in tasks previously reserved for paid staff. The complexity of the job mix has changed, as organisations have developed more short-term volunteer jobs; jobs which require a lesser time commitment and greater flexibility to meet the needs and interests of the short-term volunteer.

The Volunteer Manager is usually responsible both for designing the overall puzzle shape and for fitting together the individual pieces that complete the puzzle. This has to be done in concert with both the staff, who help design the parameters, and the volunteers, who help determine the design of individual jobs.

The overall square shape of the puzzle represents the total universe of work that the organisation desires to be accomplished through the work of volunteers.

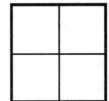

Within that square are the individual pieces of jobs that are to be done by specific volunteers, with each piece representing a volunteer.

RATIONALES FOR A VOLUNTEER PROGRAMME

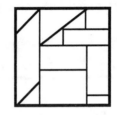

For the typical organisation today, the puzzle more closely resembles a jigsaw puzzle, one that changes shape every week.

The first step in designing a volunteer programme is to decide why the organisation wishes to involve volunteers. This decision will:

◆ determine the types of jobs and responsibilities that the organisation will create for volunteers;
◆ enable the organisation to better explain to volunteers how and why they are contributing to the work of the organisation;
◆ enable the organisation to better explain to staff why volunteers are being sought;
◆ enable the organisation to develop a plan for evaluating how effective their use of volunteers has been.

Reaching agreement on a rationale

It is highly desirable that some consensus agreement among organisation leadership and line staff is reached on this rationale. In a sense, the rationale will represent part of the mission of the volunteer programme. It will provide a quick and clear understanding of what benefit the organisation thinks will be derived from using volunteers, and give a sense of purpose to the volunteer programme. In essence, it should answer the question, *"Why are we doing this?".*

This is particularly important where there is, or appears to be, a substitution of paid work.

Potential rationales

There are many reasons for involving volunteers.

1. Providing an outreach to the community.
2. Supplementing staff resources and experiences; adding value to the organisation and its work.
3. Substituting for a paid job when the resources not there to make a staff appointment.
4. Allowing a channel for community input.
5. Giving a personal touch in services to clients.
6. Building links with other groups.
7. Assisting in fundraising efforts.
8. Cost-effectiveness in service delivery.
9. Allowing quick reaction to changing needs or crisis situations.
10. Responding to a request by someone to do something useful for the cause.

The consensus agreement should then be written down, to be provided to volunteers and staff. The example given is from the British Red Cross, and reflects not only the importance of volunteers to the organisation, but of letting the volunteers know how much their contribution is valued.

A Summary of the Volunteering Policy of the British Red Cross

Without volunteers, the British Red Cross could not exist. Volunteers are our main workforce. Supported by salaried staff, they deliver our services to the public and govern the Society at every level. British Red Cross volunteers have opportunities to exercise every talent, enthusiasm or skill and to influence and direct work and policy in all areas.

It is vital that we attract – and keep – volunteers. The Volunteering Policy recommends steps, which everyone in the British Red Cross can put into practice now, to welcome new people to the Society and reinforce the commitment and enjoyment of current volunteers.

Volunteering works best when it is based on clear and mutual benefit. People volunteer for many reasons, but everyone who volunteers wants to be valued, treated with consideration and given every opportunity for fulfilment or personal growth through their volunteering.

All volunteers should know about the many opportunities that the British Red Cross offers them, and what we expect from them in return.

INVOLVING STAFF IN DESIGNING THE VOLUNTEER PROGRAMME

It is essential to involve all levels of staff throughout the volunteer programme design process . If volunteers are going to be working in conjunction with paid staff, whether for them, alongside them or in support of them, it is vital that staff are in agreement about the purpose and worth of the volunteer job and the volunteer programme as a whole.

Staff who do not want to work with volunteers can destroy a volunteer effort, either through direct opposition or indifference. If staff are not willing to cooperate in developing realistic jobs for volunteers, if they ignore volunteers or give them second class status in the organisation, if they indicate by word or action that volunteers are a hindrance, then volunteers will quickly become disillusioned and de-motivated. They will find other causes and other organisations for which to volunteer, or they may stop volunteering altogether.

Surveying staff attitudes

One method of assessing staff attitudes is to conduct a survey. This can be done either through in-person interviewing or a printed questionnaire, and should ascertain the following points.

The level of experience of staff working with volunteers

- ◆ Have they supervised volunteers before?
- ◆ Have they ever worked in an organisation which used volunteers?
- ◆ Do they volunteer themselves?

Staff attitudes to the use of volunteers

- ◆ Are there jobs that staff feel volunteers should not be doing? If so, why?

◆ Are there programme elements, such as additional staff training, which should be instituted before volunteers are brought in?

Fears that staff might have about the use of volunteers

◆ Are there potential difficulties, such as organisational liability, or quality control questions that should be addressed?

◆ Are there worries about loss of staff jobs?

The responses to the survey should tell the volunteer manager how staff are likely to react to the inclusion of volunteers, a topic which is discussed in greater depth in the chapter on Volunteer-Staff Relationships.

Top management support

It is also desirable to have the support of the organisation's top management. This support might be represented by the official adoption by the trustees, management committee or executive committee of the organisation, of a policy supporting the use of volunteers, or by a position statement on volunteers approved by the chief staff of the organisation. One essential element of this support is that the top management and senior staff should have a clear vision of how the volunteer programme will contribute to the achievement of the organisation's mission. Some key questions that top management should consider when contemplating the creation of the volunteer programme include:

◆ how would you describe the mission of the organisation and how do you see volunteers aiding in the fulfilment of that mission?

◆ what is it that leads the organisation to consider starting a volunteer programme?

◆ what specific goals are envisioned for the volunteer programme during its first year of operation?

◆ what kind of resources is the organisation willing to invest in involving volunteers?

◆ what type of return does the organisation see itself getting from the use of volunteers?

It is important to note, however, that while it is desirable to have top management support for the use of volunteers, it is not desirable to have that support become coercive. It is not advisable for management to compel staff to use volunteers. Opposing staff can too easily drive volunteers away or make it impossible for volunteers to be successful. What is desirable is an attitude by top management that encourages staff and rewards effective use of volunteer resources; an approach using the carrot and not the stick.

ORGANISATIONAL CLIMATE

The overall organisational climate will also influence how volunteers can be involved. Volunteers will quickly become aware of attitudes within the organisation, whether about how well the organisation is doing, how things are done, or who and what is important to the organisation. These sometimes subtle cues regarding the organisation's style and methods will influence the volunteer in deciding whether the organisation is worth their time. Since the organisation will often become a work place for the volunteers, they are more likely to appreciate and stay at an organisation which has a positive environment. What is needed is a sense of common mission and purpose, and an understanding that productive steps are being taken towards its accomplishment.

Evidence of a good organisational climate includes:

◆ a clear sense of individual roles, with respect for roles of others
◆ a willingness to sacrifice for a goal
◆ trust
◆ tolerance and acceptance
◆ open and honest communication
◆ group identity: 'we're in this together'
◆ inclusion, not exclusion
◆ mutual support and interdependence.

An organisational climate which is favourable toward volunteers will communicate two feelings or attitudes to the volunteers.

Acceptance: the volunteers are welcomed by and connected with the overall purpose and operation of the organisation.

Appreciation: that each volunteer has a unique, recognised contribution to make to the purpose and operation of the organisation.

PERSONNEL MANAGEMENT

Policies and procedures

Volunteer programme management also requires the creation of some formal rules and procedures. After determining why volunteers are to be used, the organisation will need to develop its own set of policies and procedures governing the employment of volunteers.

The policies will allow the volunteer manager to develop a consistent pattern of volunteer use, and will provide assistance in dealing with problem situations. Both the policies, and the procedures by which they will be implemented, should be developed in conjunction with staff, particularly if the organisation is using volunteers in a variety of different projects. Some samples of volunteer policies are provided in Appendix A.

If you have a question about the content of a policy or procedure, refer to the policies and procedures that the organisation uses for paid staff. The rules should be as similar as possible: 'when in doubt, copy'.

Forms and records

The volunteer programme will also need to develop some basic personnel-related systems. Volunteer programmes operate with the essential forms required for any operation involving people:

◆ intake forms
◆ job description
◆ contracts of employment
◆ evaluation instruments.

Individual records need to be maintained for each volunteer, giving:

◆ their biographical and contact information
◆ records of their positions and training
◆ hours contributed and tasks accomplished
◆ expenses claimed and reimbursed
◆ dates of connection with the organisation.

The systems and files developed should match those of paid staff, and can often be the same forms.

Investigate the use of computer software packages to assist in these personnel functions. Software packages are now available (or can be custom developed for your organisation) that will greatly aid you in keeping track of the names, skills, interests, and availability of your volunteers. They can also assist you in performing the paperwork functions of volunteer management, conserving your time to deal with those parts of the job which require human contact.

EVALUATION

The plan for the volunteer programme should also consider the process by which the volunteer's contribution is to be evaluated. The design of the programme operations should include the information systems which will enable staff, management, volunteers, and the volunteer manager to determine how things are going and whether things can be improved.

The intent of evaluation is both to uncover problems (low rates of volunteer retention; need for additional training) and to reward accomplishment. Much like individuals, organisations and programmes need to know when they are successful; without measurements of achievement it is impossible to know when you have succeeded.

In developing the evaluation plan, consider the following questions:

◆ *What would volunteers like to know about themselves, or about the programme?*

Hours contributed, benefits to clients, responsibilities and so on.

◆ *What would staff who work with volunteers like to know?*

Numbers of volunteers in their area, number of clients served, and so on.

◆ *What would top management like to know?*

Who is utilising volunteers, value of volunteer time donated, and so on.

◆ *What would the volunteer manager like to know?*

Where volunteers are coming from, rate of volunteer turnover, and so on.

ASSESSING YOUR PLAN

Assess your plan for involving volunteers by reviewing the following checklist. If you have not completed the items on the list, then you still have preparations to finish before you and your organisation can effectively initiate a volunteer programme.

◆ Have you consulted with the staff who will be working with each volunteer?

◆ Are these staff clear on what their role will be in working with the volunteer?

◆ Is a complete and accurate job description written for the volunteer position?

Operate by these rules:

◆ *Think first and get volunteers later. They'll appreciate your consideration.*

◆ *Do it right the first time; it's easier than having to do it over again.*

◆ Does this job description clearly identify the qualifications for the position and outline both the purpose and nature of the work to be done?

◆ Have you established a good working environment for the volunteer, in terms of supervisory relationships, workspace and equipment?

◆ Do you have a plan for seeking qualified applicants for the positions?

◆ Do you know how you will distinguish qualified applicants from unqualified applicants? Do you know what you will do with unqualified applicants?

◆ Do you have a plan for orienting and training volunteers?

Resist the impulse to initiate a volunteer effort too quickly. The time spent in planning and preparation will greatly reduce confusion and any problems that may arise later.

CHAPTER FOUR

Creating Motivating Volunteer Jobs

Before recruiting volunteers you need to have a clear understanding of the duties they are to carry out, ensuring that the roles have been clearly defined. This process is one of the most important functions of the volunteer manager: without good jobs, the organisation will have nothing of value to offer volunteers. Organisations that can offer interesting and productive jobs will find it easier to attract and keep volunteers than organisations with boring or unsatisfactory jobs. This chapter explains the steps to producing a volunteer job description.

Topics covered include:

♦ **Involvement of members of staff**

♦ **Design of the job and level of responsibility**

♦ **Volunteer job descpritions**

♦ **Matching jobs to volunteers**

STAFF INVOLVEMENT

In an organisation employing staff, a volunteer manager should begin the process of creating volunteer jobs by gaining staff involvement. The role of the volunteer manager in job development is thus one of consulting with staff, helping them develop volunteer jobs where they can provide support, and jobs that volunteers want to do. During the process, the volunteer manager interviews staff to determine how they might best involve volunteers. This interview does not consist merely of asking staff what jobs they might have for a volunteer because that is unlikely to provoke a creative response from staff who have no experience working with volunteers.

Instead, the volunteer manager should take staff through a process (first developed by Ivan Scheier) in which they are encouraged to answer the following questions:

♦ *What are the parts of your job that you really like to do?*

Staff responses might include activities such as working directly with clients, doing research, or public speaking.

♦ *What are the parts of your job that you dislike?*

Responses might include compiling reports, writing the organisation newsletter, or filing.

◆ *What other activities or projects have you always wanted to do but never had the time for?*

Responses might include working with a new client group, investigating new sources of funding, or starting a programme in a new community.

◆ *What are the things you would like to see done that no one has the skills to do?*

Responses might include upgrading the organisation's computer capability, doing market research, or creating a new organisation logo.

The answers to these questions can form the basis for defining volunteer jobs that can be integrated with the staff workload and which will be supported by staff. If the volunteer manager can bring in a volunteer who will relieve staff members of the tasks they don't enjoy, thereby giving them time to do the things they've always wanted to do, staff have a powerful incentive to make sure that the volunteer has a good experience at the organisation. In this way the volunteer manager develops volunteer work that is both real (i.e. it really needs to be done) and will be appreciated by the staff. Consequently, the potential for staff-volunteer difficulties, such as staff forgetting to thank volunteers for their efforts, is greatly reduced.

The interview process described here can also be utilised to educate staff as to the correct 'shape' for a volunteer job request, as will be discussed later in this chapter. By helping the staff develop the volunteer job description, the volunteer coordinator will greatly lessen the prospect of being bombarded with impossible requests for volunteers: 'Someone to come in from 10-5, Monday through Friday, to do my filing'.

The circle of staff needs

The process of staff involvement should be a continuous one. The volunteer manager should develop a

---

Consulting tools

The volunteer programme manager can employ a number of tools to show staff what will be possible. A menu approach, giving staff lists of possibilities, is often effective. The tools include:

1. A list of the types of jobs/functions that volunteers are already performing in the organisation.

2. A list of types of jobs/functions that volunteers perform in other organisations in the community or in similar programmes across the country.

3. Skills/descriptions of available volunteers.

These listings will serve to provide ideas on potential jobs to staff who do not have a clear understanding of the potential uses of volunteers within the organisation, and should broaden the perspective and improve the creativity of staff in developing interesting and challenging volunteer positions.

process for on-going communication with staff, either by periodic follow-up interviews or through written communication, in which the process of new job development continues. One method for accomplishing this is to institute a 'work wanted' section in the organisation newsletter or via a memo to all staff, in which volunteer jobs are highlighted, or in which the skills of new volunteers are announced. The aim of this communication is to create a demand for additional types of volunteer effort.

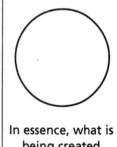

In essence, what is being created through this process is the circle of staff needs

The circle represents the universe of needs and interests of the staff, formatted into a request for particular work to be done. The circle includes a request for:

◆ specific skills that are needed;

◆ the time commitment that is required;

◆ attitudes and other qualities that represent what the organisation is looking for in a volunteer.

DESIGNING VOLUNTEER JOBS FOR RESULTS

Volunteer jobs that are boring and unsatisfying lead to a high turnover of volunteers; interesting, challenging and rewarding jobs lead to enthusiasm and good results. The difference between the two depends in part on the person doing the job; different people have different motivational needs and will find different jobs interesting. An often overlooked source of this difference, however, lies in the design of the job itself.

The cornerstone of all successful programmes is placing volunteers in jobs they look forward to, which should ensure stability and high morale. Job descriptions for volunteers in most organisations look exactly like those of paid staff. The jobs tend to be designed around the standard management practices of the non-volunteer world. However, while paid people will do a job that is unrewarding because they are compensated for doing it, volunteers will not do so for long. This has given volunteers in general a reputation for being unreliable, because if the volunteer does not find the job to be personally satisfying, they will probably choose to leave. To attract and retain volunteers, you must design jobs they want to do. Therefore, when you design jobs for volunteers you might more productively heed the principles of those who design games.

Games are voluntary activities that are designed to be interesting, exciting and motivating. Games are so motivating, in fact, that people will spend their time and money on expensive equipment and lessons in order to get better at them, something that is rarely true of work.

The point here is not that volunteering should be a game, but that it should have the same motivational qualities that games have. All games have four characteristics that work can also have but seldom does:

◆ ownership

◆ the authority to think

◆ responsibility for the results or outcomes

◆ keeping score.

When you design volunteer jobs, therefore, it is good to try to include these characteristics. Jobs designed with these characteristics also require less supervisory effort.

Ownership

By ownership, we mean that the volunteer has a sense of personal responsibility for something. Their job contains something they can point to and say 'This is mine'. This might be a particular product, event or geographic area. In the non-profit world, the ownership is often the client that a volunteer is helping or the project they are working on. There are many examples of volunteers having such responsibility: carers, helpline operators, advisors in a crisis clinic, and youth workers are all volunteers who have one or more clients that are theirs.

Ownership is removed when volunteers do only one of many activities the organisation provides as part of its service. In some social care organisations, for example, volunteers might do a preliminary screening of client needs, then hand over to a trained professional who would offer specific advice or determine eligibility for services. When volunteers merely do one activity in a string of activities, they can lose the intense satisfaction of helping others that drives most volunteer efforts. Although they know that somewhere down the line they have contributed to clients' needs, their sense of pride and ownership in this is diluted by all the others who have had a hand in it.

Ownership gives the volunteer something to be in charge of and hence to be proud of. Giving volunteers a project of their own that they can control is particularly important for today's new breed of volunteer, who is less interested in making a long-term commitment to an organisation than volunteers used to be. Short term, specific projects are therefore particularly important in attracting new volunteers.

As an example, volunteers fixing up a school will get more satisfaction if they do everything towards refurbishing a particular room than if they do one activity (such as painting or washing windows) in all the rooms. The first circumstance provides them with a sense of ownership ('This is my room') whereas in the second case, the sense of ownership and responsibility is diluted, causing volunteers to become bored and leave sooner than those who have full responsibility for a client or a project.

This is not to say that teamwork should be avoided in job design. Teams of people can also feel a sense of ownership. In this example, there could be a sense that the school belongs to the group. In one US city, there is an all-volunteer programme which was formed when the parks department reduced its complement of paid maintenance staff. Teams of volunteers have parks which they keep free of litter and graffiti, and the sense of ownership is met because the team can look at their park and take pride in its appearance.

The authority to think

The difference between a team and a collection of isolated individuals is that a team has the authority to plan and evaluate its work and agree on who is going to do what. This authority to think is the second key element in good job design, whether for individuals or teams. With this authority the individual or group not only does the work but plays some part in deciding how to do it.

Volunteer managers tend to resist allowing volunteers this authority. The volunteer may work only a few hours per month and so have difficulty keeping up with what is going on. Also, standard management practice holds that it is the supervisor's job to do the planning and the employee's job to carry out whatever has been decided.

Indeed, when a volunteer first comes on board, this may be the most comfortable way to proceed. As volunteers learn the job, however, the fact that they are only doing what someone else decides begins to sap their motivation and dilute their feelings of pride in what they accomplish. They will tend either to resent being told what to do, or to lose interest in the job. Either of these will increase the likelihood of their dropping out.

This does not mean abdicating your responsibility for ensuring good results from volunteers. Obviously, you can't afford to have all your volunteers doing whatever they think is best, and without guidance. You need to make sure that they are all working toward the achievement of a coordinated and agreed set of goals. What you can do, however, is involve them in the planning and deciding process so that they do feel a sense of authority over how their job is done.

The process of managing all this is explained in detail in the section on empowering volunteers. For now, suffice it to say that in designing the job you should ask:

◆ how would a person who tells the volunteer what to do know what to tell them?

◆ what does the volunteer's supervisor do to figure out what to tell the volunteer to do?'

You can then include those thinking tasks in the volunteer's job description, healing the schism between thinking and doing. In a sense, in doing this, you give the volunteer back their brain.

Responsibility for results

The third critical element in developing a work structure that encourages excellence is to make sure that the volunteers are responsible for achieving specific results, rather than simply performing a set of activities. If they are focused on the end product or goal they will get the satisfaction of making progress toward a meaningful end. A crime prevention volunteer in a Neighbourhood Watch scheme, for example, will experience more satisfaction if their goal is to reduce burglaries to a specific, achievable number, than if their job is simply knocking on doors to talk to people about security.

Most job descriptions for volunteers are not defined in terms of results. Instead, they merely list a series of activities the volunteer is supposed to perform. The result is rarely mentioned. In fact, the responsibility is sometimes fragmented between a number of people, and the individual volunteer loses sight of the result. As a direct consequence of this, results are poorly and inefficiently obtained and the volunteer gets bored.

At first it can be difficult to grasp the concept of defining jobs in terms of results, so let us look at some examples. A volunteer in a drug abuse programme, for example, may be told that his job is to spend three hours per week counselling a client. This is a statement of an activity to be performed. No result of the counselling has been specified, and if the volunteer doesn't achieve much, we shouldn't be surprised. The job appears to require no particular skill or effort, other than sitting in a room with someone for three hours. To define the result, you would need to ask, 'what is the outcome we want from the counselling? What do we want the volunteer to accomplish in these three hours per week?'. The answer would probably be something like 'clients will be able to cope with daily life without resorting to the use of drugs'. By defining this desired result for the volunteer, you offer a challenging and worthwhile accomplishment for the volunteer to be working towards.

Volunteers in a school programme might be asked to work with children on reading skills. When you ask only that someone work with the children, you are not creating any responsibility for helping the children learn. There is no challenge in the job when it is defined in this way. It is better to specify the skill improvements that the volunteer is responsible for helping the child achieve. The job description thus might read something like 'bring the child up to age 6 reading ability'.

Defining volunteer jobs in terms of results helps to meet people's need for a sense of achievement or accomplishment. It helps them feel that their volunteer activity is valuable and worthwhile. It also helps the volunteer programme operate more effectively. When people know what they are supposed to accomplish, they are more likely to do so. It makes sense that you should let them know what results are expected and then hold the volunteers responsible for accomplishing them.

Keeping score

The fourth critical element in good job design is to decide how to measure to what degree results are being achieved. If you don't do this, the statement of result will fail to have any motivating value, and it will be impossible for both volunteer and supervisor to know how well the volunteer is doing.

Many volunteer managers shy away from measuring volunteer performance, thinking that doing so would discourage or demotivate them. The opposite is more likely to be the case. If people can't tell how well they are doing, or if they are succeeding or failing, they tend to get bored with the activity. There is also no incentive to try a different course of action, if you don't know that your present course isn't working.

For some jobs the measure of performance is fairly obvious and easy to state. In the case of a crime prevention volunteer, for example, the number of burglaries in her area is a readily available statistical measure. We can use these statistics (provided she is responsible for the same geographic area for which statistics are being compiled) to measure her achievement. Every time a burglary occurs in her area, she will naturally ask 'what could have been done to prevent that?'. These thoughts spur creativity, and encourage new, and hopefully, even more effective approaches. If her job is merely defined as engraving personal identification numbers on people's stereos, however, and there is no feedback to her on how well the scheme is doing, there is little likelihood that more effective approaches will be tried.

Although many don't, all volunteer managers should take time to decide how to monitor volunteer progress and results. However, even those managers who do measure performance tend to measure the wrong things. They keep track of things such as hours worked or miles driven or client contacts made. These measures tend to lack any real meaning because they do not tell us whether the volunteer is accomplishing anything of value. They do not measure whether the result is being achieved.

To determine how to measure a given result, involve the volunteers who do the job, by asking:

◆ what information would tell us if you are succeeding in achieving the result?

◆ how could we collect this information?

Measuring performance makes it possible to introduce an element of competition. It is possible to set targets, to encourage these targets to be surpassed, and even to set records. Records are tremendously motivating. Every day people do ridiculous things to break records, such as making an omelette that weighs four tons. The Guinness Book of Records lists some of these incredible achievements. If people spend time and effort to do such silly things, voluntarily, think of the work they might do if there were records to set for something more serious!

VOLUNTEER JOB DESCRIPTIONS

Each volunteer should have a written job description, and this should be developed jointly by the Volunteer Coordinator and the staff member who will supervise the volunteer. It provides a summary of the work and activities to be performed by the volunteer and functions as an instrument for supervision and evaluation.

The ability to write a good job description is useful. In some ways, job descriptions are more important for volunteer staff than for paid staff. Paid staff are accustomed to learning their job by osmosis – coming to work and spending time watching what is happening and determining what they should be doing and how they should be working. For a volunteer, this learning period may be impractical, since ten days of on-the-job learning can easily translate into several weeks or even months for a part-time volunteer. Unless the organisation is prepared for the volunteer to begin work immediately and has prepared suitable instructions, the volunteer can be discouraged right from the start. A job description which accurately represents the tasks to be undertaken and the effort that is required can serve to ready the organisation for the appearance of the volunteer. If you discover that either you or the staff with whom the volunteer will be working cannot put together a precise job description, then it would be better to re-initiate the process of job development than to recruit a volunteer for a position which cannot be properly defined.

A good job description will contain the following elements:

Title: What the job will be called, or what position is being offered.

Purpose: The result the job is to accomplish. This is the most important part of the job description.

Suggested Activities: Examples of what might be done to accomplish the purpose. The word suggested indicates that the volunteer has some authority to think, to pursue other approved activities if their supervisor agrees these might be effective in achieving the result.

Measures: How you will tell if the result is being achieved.

Qualifications: What skills, attitudes, and knowledge are desired, as well as any requirements regarding dress or conduct.

Time: Estimated number of hours, length of commitment, and flexibility in scheduling.

Site: Location of work.

Supervision: Relationships with staff and other volunteers, reporting requirements and supervisory relationships, as well as procedures for monitoring and dealing with problems.

Benefits: Training, insurance, parking, reimbursement of expenses, child care provision, any volunteer remuneration, events to thank volunteers, and so on.

An additional item to include might be the values and philosophy of the organisation that the volunteer is expected to adhere to. The precise format of the job description is not important. What is important is that all of the elements are covered and that, in particular, a well thought out purpose be defined for the volunteer.

WRITING AN EFFECTIVE JOB DESCRIPTION A CASE STUDY

There are four essential principles of a well-designed job: ownership, authority to think, responsibility for results, and keeping score.

In the US, there is a volunteer programme whose main purpose is to do household chores for handicapped and elderly people who might otherwise be institutionalised. Originally, the volunteer job description wasn't even in writing. Volunteers were simply told to do whatever cleaning and home maintenance the paid social worker deemed necessary. The programme was plagued with a high turnover rate, as volunteers often found the work more unpleasant than they had expected.

In terms of our four criteria, the volunteers did have ownership – they had clients who were their own and no one else's. But they had little control over what they did, as the social worker limited them to a certain list of tasks. There was no clear end result and they were measured only by whether they completed their assigned tasks.

In redesigning the job, the staff member responsible for supervision and the volunteer coordinator, sat down with a group of volunteers to define results and measures. At this day-long meeting, two desired outcomes were identified. The first was that clients would be able to stay in their homes as long as they had no serious medical problems that made institutionalisation necessary. This result was easily measured by the number of non-medical institutionalisations. Such a result didn't seem enough for the volunteers involved since they felt this could be easily achieved. They suggested that a second outcome be included; that clients' houses be clean. This brought up the problem of how to measure whether a house was clean, since people have different standards of acceptable cleanliness. After much discussion, the group finally decided that the client should be the one to determine if the house was clean or not. The final statement of this second result was *'Clients will be satisfied with the cleanliness of their homes'*.

Determining how to measure this second outcome raised two key questions: *'What information will tell us that we are doing a good job?'* and *'How will we collect it?'*. As in most cases, the answer was implied by the desired outcome itself. The information required was the opinion of the client. Volunteers could get this information informally by asking the client at the end of their visit whether they were satisfied. The programme also solicited the opinions of clients on a more formal basis, through a monthly survey. The results of this survey, in terms of numbers of satisfied clients, was then fed back to the volunteers.

Within the framework of what would be deemed acceptable results, the volunteer was then given the authority to do the thinking necessary to achieve them. Instead of the social worker figuring out what needed to be done, the volunteer was given the responsibility to work this out with the client. Their success was measured by the degree to which they achieved the two results. Where volunteers were having difficulty achieving client satisfaction, they naturally turned to their supervisor for help and advice as to what they should do differently.

This change in the way the job was defined had a transforming effect on all concerned. The social worker was relieved of the enormous burden of determining what chores needed to be done for each client, and was able to concentrate on actually doing social work. This made them happier and, because they were able to work personally with individual clients, it also resulted in a reduction in the number of clients who complained – because complaining was the only way they knew how to cope with their loneliness.

The volunteers got greater satisfaction from their work, as they were responsible not just for doing odious chores but for keeping their clients out of a nursing home – a much more rewarding role. They had the authority to devise ways of accomplishing this and of cleaning the homes to the clients' satisfaction. And they had clear measures of whether they were achieving their results. Because of all this, volunteer turnover was greatly reduced, and the volunteer programme developed a reputation for good client service.

In this scenario, the volunteer director's role also changed. Instead of assigning volunteers to clients and then trying desperately to keep them interested in doing the task (by organising recognition dinners, providing certificates of appreciation, giving motivational talks, and other highly time-consuming measures), they were now a person volunteers sought out whenever they thought they weren't achieving their results. Recruiting time was also greatly reduced due to a much lower volunteer turnover.

Here is an excerpt from the final job description:

Title:
Senior Service Aide

Purpose:
Clients will be able to remain in their own homes.
Clients will be satisfied with the tidiness and cleanliness of their homes.

Suggested Activities:

◆ identify tasks clients can't do themselves and want done

◆ describe tasks clients cannot do to the supervisor and seek approval for performing them

◆ devise ways clients can do more for themselves

◆ complete approved household chores

Measures:

◆ client response on periodic survey

◆ number of client compliments and complaints

Qualifications:

Skills in listening and the ability to communicate well with a variety of people is essential.

Time:

Must be able to devote four hours per week for a minimum of two months. Scheduling will be made to meet the availability of the volunteer as long as it is convenient for the client.

Site:

Volunteers will work in the homes of their individual client.

Supervision:

Volunteers will report to the Senior Service supervisor in their area. Their daily work will not be closely supervised.

Benefits:

Volunteers will receive training in elements of gerontology and in household cleaning as needed. While on the job, volunteers will have full liability insurance. Mileage will be reimbursed at a rate of 50p per mile. Other out-of-pocket expenses will also be reimbursed. A work record will be kept for each volunteer so that the position will provide them with good job references. Regular social events such as pot-lucks are held for volunteers at which they are recognised for their valuable contributions.

Negotiating and Updating

While the job description ought to be formally constructed before recruiting volunteers, it should not be considered an immutable, finished document. Volunteer programmes only succeed when volunteers are motivated to do the job. To ensure this, the job description needs to adapt to meet the needs of the volunteer.

As the interviewer attempts to match the job to the needs and interests of potential volunteers, some negotiation may take place. Further negotiation should take place after the volunteer has been accepted and has begun work. As the volunteer gains more familiarity with the actual work to be done, they may make suggestions as to how the job might be modified to make it even more rewarding.

As Ivan Scheier pointed out fifteen years ago, this is in some sense the opposite of what you do with paid staff. There you expect the person to accommodate him or herself to the job. With volunteers, you need to accommodate the job to the individual; to build jobs volunteers want to do.

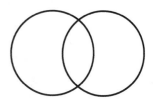

These circles represent the needs of the organisation and the motivational needs of the volunteer. The area where the two circles overlap represents the volunteer job which will both benefit the organisation and be suitable for the individual volunteer.

A second circle *(above)* can then be added to the circle of staff needs discussed at the beginning of this chapter. This is the circle of what volunteers want to do. Where there is overlap between the circles, where volunteers are doing things they want to do and that staff want done, we have the building blocks of a strong volunteer programme.

CHAPTER FIVE
Recruitment

Recruitment of volunteers can be difficult, because you are not offering them any financial benefit. However, if you recruit the right volunteers, they will provide your organisation not only with an extra resource, but with motivated, committed advocates. This chapter details the stages of recruiting the right volunteer – for the benefit of your organisation and for their own personal benefit.

MEETING THE NEEDS OF POTENTIAL VOLUNTEERS

As discussed in the previous chapter, volunteers will only give their time if they are motivated to do so. This means that recruitment is not a process of persuading a person into an activity they didn't want to do. Rather, it should be seen as the process of showing people they can do something they already want to do.

In recruiting volunteers, you want to find people who are attracted by the challenge of achieving the results outlined in the volunteer job description. You might picture the process of matching two sets of needs – those of the volunteer and those of the organisation. In chapter four, it was emphasised that good volunteer jobs are created by identifying the needs and aspirations of staff. Now you need to construct a *circle of volunteer needs*, representing those things which a volunteer might want from an organisation, including such items as interesting work, flexibility, or recognition.

Topics covered include:

- ◆ **Meeting the needs of the volunteer**
- ◆ **Recruiting methods**
- ◆ **Recruiting in difficult areas**
- ◆ **Recruiting groups of volunteers**
- ◆ **Overcoming volunteer's concerns**
- ◆ **Identifying the positive aspects of the job**

This circle can be constructed for each volunteer, because each individual will have different needs and motivations.

The recruitment process then becomes an effort to identify and reach those volunteers whose circle of needs are congruent with what the organisation wants, those whose motivational needs can be met by the volunteer position you are offering. It is essential to remember that the recruitment process begins, and in many ways hinges upon, the creation of a good volunteer job. If you ask a person 'What would it take to get you to volunteer some of your time for this organisation?', the answers you get tend not to be about the recruitment technique but about the type of job you are offering. Nearly all will say something like '*It would have to be an interesting job*', or '*It would have to be something that I felt was worthwhile*', or '*It should be work that allowed me to develop as a person*'. Attempting to recruit volunteers without first having designed worthwhile jobs for them is equivalent to attempting to sell a product to people who have no need for it.

The recruitment process might be pictured as a 'funnel'. It is the process of identifying and separating from the entire universe of potential volunteers (the whole population of your community) those who best fit the needs of the organisation and its work.

Organisations recruiting volunteers may suffer from two very different recruitment problems. One problem, which is universally feared by new volunteer managers, is that of not having enough volunteers. The second problem, which is much more subtle and yet much more common, is of not having enough of the right volunteers, and, indeed, of having too many of the wrong ones.

Effective recruiting consists of attracting just enough of the right volunteers. This distinction is an important one, with significant implications for a volunteer manager. Inexperienced volunteer managers often think that it is desirable to have large numbers of people seeking voluntary work with their organisation. Unfortunately, in practice, a surplus of volunteers can cause difficulties. If you advertise for volunteers and only have room for two, what do you do if twenty apply? Initially, you must expend significant amounts of time in the screening and interviewing process, determining which of the volunteers should be accepted. Then you must reject most of the volunteers, risking the prospect of their becoming resentful. The only thing worse than having to reject volunteers is accepting their service when you don't really have work for them, at which point they will become convinced that you and the organisation are incompetent.

Recruitment, then, is a matter of proportion; balancing the need for applicants with the work required to separate the qualified from the unqualified.

Guidelines for involving volunteers

REACH is the charity which finds part-time, expenses only jobs for retired – or otherwise available – business and professional people who want to use their skills as volunteers anywhere in the United Kingdom. It issues the following guidelines for organisations looking to involve its volunteers.

DO

1. **Define the job.** Be clear why you are recruiting at this level and what the volunteer will be doing. Volunteers will be keener to join your organisation if they feel that there is a worthwhile job to be done. Many REACH volunteers have held senior positions and could make a major contribution. Think big!

2. **Involve your other workers**. Get their views on the organisation's needs and keep them informed. Their good-will and co-operation are essential if the volunteer is to integrate successfully with the team.

3. **Describe the job realistically**. Make it sound attractive, certainly, but be honest about its limitations and any special difficulties the volunteer can expect to meet. Jobs inaccurately portrayed have a good chance of failure.

4. **Interview selectively**. Allow time for this. You need to establish that the candidate has the personality, skills and availability to meet your requirements and fit in with your other workers, as well as to sort out the practical details.

5. **Take up references**. Always useful, but essential if the volunteer will be working with vulnerable groups or have access to money or confidential information. You may gain valuable insight into the individual and will be protecting your organisation's interests.

6. **Agree a probationary period**. Fairer to all parties. Gives you both the opportunity to see if the appointment is working, and allows either side to withdraw gracefully if it is not.

7. **Brief your volunteers well**. Give them every opportunity to learn about your organisation by introductory discussions, training sessions and any other means which will help to further their knowledge and understanding, and thereby increase their commitment to the cause.

8. **Support your volunteers**. They need to know to whom they are responsible, what independent action they may take, and where they can turn for assistance. Ensure that they have adequate working facilities and access to information.

9. **Reimburse expenses and provide insurance cover**. Volunteers are entitled to expect these. No one should be out of pocket as a result of working for you – volunteers give their time and effort, not their money. The amount of expenses, and arrangement for payment, should be agreed beforehand and confirmed in writing.

DON'T

1. **Replace a paid worker by a volunteer.** This causes resentment among workers and may even get you into trouble with the unions.

2. **Expect results too quickly**. Although you may have recruited people authoritative in their own fields, remember that your volunteers may have been used to very different working practices, and may well suffer from culture shock in the new environment. As confidence grows, you may be surprised at the acquisition of unexpected skills and the increased contribution that they can make.

3. **Waste talent**. Use the volunteer's skills for which you had recruited them, even if you are short of staff. Most people are willing to help out with routine tasks in an emergency, but do not make a habit of such demands since they will soon result in dissatisfied volunteers.

4. **Take on someone you do not need**. Nothing is more dispiriting to volunteers and loses them quicker than not having enough to do. Volunteers, like the rest of us, need to be needed – perhaps even more so, since they are not getting paid for what they do.

HOW TO RECRUIT VOLUNTEERS

Warm body recruitment

Warm body recruitment is effective when you are recruiting for a volunteer position that can be done by most people, either because no special skills are required or because almost anyone can be taught the necessary skills in a short time. Examples of volunteer jobs suitable for warm body recruitment include a 'hugger' at a Special Olympics event, or a worker in an information booth. Warm body recruitment is particularly effective when seeking large numbers of volunteers for short-term simple jobs, such as helping at a special event, like a festival or a fun run.

How to recruit volunteers

There are three different volunteer recruitment processes that can be used.

1 Warm body recruitment

2 Targeting recruitment

3 Concentric circle recruitment

Each is quite different in what it seeks to accomplish and in what it is effective in accomplishing.

Methods for warm body recruitment

Warm body recruitment consists of spreading the message about the potential volunteer position to as broad an audience as possible. The theory is that somewhere among this audience will be enough people who find this work interesting.

The primary methods for warm body recruitment are:

♦ distribution of organisation brochures or posters advertising the need for volunteers;

♦ use of public television, radio or newspaper advertisements or publicity;

♦ contacting local groups such as a community organisation or the Scouts which might provide the person power.

Distribution of organisation brochures

There are a great number of possible sites for distribution of printed information. The aim is to place brochures in locations where people are likely to pick them up and read them, or where people can actually use the brochures to advise those who come to seek their advice. Possible sites include:

♦ job centres and employment bureaux

♦ libraries

♦ tourist information centres

◆ chambers of commerce
◆ school and youth clubs
◆ church bulletin boards
◆ community centres
◆ volunteer bureaux
◆ hospital waiting rooms and clinics
◆ shop windows.

Those programmes which deliver a service within an identifiable neighbourhood might best benefit from a simple door-to-door distribution campaign.

Advertising

With an ad on television or radio, or a good classified ad in the local newspaper, perhaps only 0.01% of the audience will be interested. But if over one million people see the ad this could result in 100 applicants.

However, despite the efforts to involve volunteers through the mass media, it is difficult to rely on this method to solve all of your recruitment problems.

It may be difficult to describe a complicated job in the short framework of a newspaper ad or a radio or television announcement. If you do attempt to construct such an ad, you might wish to concentrate on selling the needs of your client population, since it will be simpler to describe their needs than it will be to describe the entire job. Other motivational needs which can usefully be mentioned include the provision of training or other support to the volunteer, and the availability of flexible working hours to make it easier for the volunteer to meet the requirements of the job.

It is important to realise that even if ads like these do attract a volunteer, they will not guarantee that recruitment is successful. You will still need to individually motivate the potential volunteer about the job and the work of the organisation. Mass media techniques will simply get you close enough to the volunteer to make a recruitment pitch.

Speaking to community groups

One of the best methods of warm body recruitment is to arrange presentations to local clubs and other groups. Such presentations can serve both to inform the public about what your organisation does and to recruit new volunteers. In using this method of recruitment, be sure to follow the advice below.

- Deliberately select those groups you wish to speak to. There are two main groups which can be helpful: those whose membership regularly participate in helping in the community (Rotary, service clubs, etc.), and those whose individual members are likely to have a common interest in your cause. Schedule these groups of people first.

- In seeking an opportunity to speak to the group, consider going through a group member. The member can serve as your authenticator, paving your way to a more receptive audience with the person responsible for making the decision. They can also make it more likely that you will be invited to speak. Many groups have a social secretary who is desperate to find good speakers.

- Try to time your speaking to meet both the group's and your needs. Find out about other projects the group is already committed to and time your talk to coincide with their need to develop a new project. Determine how much lead time they need and make sure that your request is not too immediate for them to meet.

- Pick your presenters carefully. Make sure the person who is speaking can explain what your organisation does and exactly what is needed from the volunteers. Consider sending a volunteer who can speak convincingly about the worth of the volunteer job.

- If possible, use a visual presentation (slides, pictures, etc.) to increase interest. If your presentation is boring, the group may assume that your jobs will be too.

- Be prepared for people to offer their services immediately. Take along brochures, examples of jobs for which they are needed, sign-up sheets, and so on. If someone expresses interest, don't leave without their name and phone number, and commit yourself to following up their interest. Follow up as soon as possible.

- Be prepared for too much success. You may need to have a back-up plan to handle the entire group wanting to volunteer. If several group members decide to volunteer, you might want to consider ways in which they might work together as a group while performing the volunteer work.

- Remember that at some point during your presentation you should directly and unequivocally ask the audience to volunteer. Very few people will insist on volunteering for your programme without being asked to do so.

Targeting recruitment

With this approach you determine the kind of person who would like to do the job and track them down. Start by examining the motivations and backgrounds of volunteers currently in the position to find out if there are any common factors. Do they have the same motivations? Do they have similar backgrounds, education, experiences or occupations? Do they come from similar groups? Did they all hear about the job in the same fashion? These common factors will enable you to identify people who might like to do the job. But remember that who you get may then be determined by how you have recruited in the past.

Research studies from the early 1990s provide examples of this approach. A study of 4-H (a US volunteer programme with youth as clients) volunteer leaders found that 4-H volunteers who continued in their leadership roles tended to differ from their discontinuing counterparts in geographical location, number of children in the family and number of children who had participated in 4-H. Other studies have found that individuals willing to work as volunteers in the field of mental retardation differ from non-volunteers in that they placed less emphasis on success (both social and economic) and greater emphasis on values such as equality, personal expression, and growth.

A targeted recruitment campaign involves answering a series of questions.

What is the job that needs to be done?

As stressed already, it is the job, the opportunity to do something that meets the volunteer's motivational needs, that is the key to attracting most volunteers. A general message, such as 'Volunteers are needed at the Crisis Clinic', doesn't let anyone know what the volunteers do there. As such, the message doesn't indicate to a potential volunteer that there is anything which they might find interesting.

Volunteer managers who send such a general message tend to do so for one or two reasons. The first is that it is so obvious to everyone in the organisation what the volunteers do that they assume the entire community is familiar with their efforts. If the organisation does a good job of community education, this may well be so, but not all potential volunteers may have got the message.

The second is that there are many things volunteers do at the organisation and it would be impossible to list them all. As you will see in the next few sections, effective recruitment must be targeted to segments of the population. Different jobs in an organisation will appeal to different people with different motivational needs. By targeting the campaign at different groups, you can stress particular jobs that will appeal to those groups and avoid a message that mentions no attractive jobs.

Who would want to do the job that needs to be done?

This is a question that most of us don't bother to ask, because we have been able to recruit successful volunteers from a variety of backgrounds. However, it is easier to recruit the right person for the job if you have answered this question, because you can target your message to the needs of that particular group. Messages sent to the community in general have to apply to everyone and often end up speaking to no one.

Ask yourself if there is a particular type of person you wish to recruit. Do you want someone from a particular age group? Do you want someone of a particular sex or ethnic background? Do you want someone with certain professional skills? The answers to these questions may be multiple – you may want young, old, and middle-aged people, for example. But if you have reached this conclusion in a thoughtful way (rather than merely saying, 'You'll take any age group'), you can then begin to target a separate recruitment campaign to each of these groups, with slightly different messages.

The advantage of sending a slightly different message to each group is that you have a better chance of speaking directly to each group's motivational needs. You will therefore tend to get a larger percentage of people from each group to consider volunteering for your organisation than you otherwise would. For example, if you identify newcomers to town as potential volunteers, you might stress jobs in which they can meet new people, and your volunteer recruiting efforts would highlight efforts in which people work as teams. If you identify harried executives as potential volunteers, on the other hand, you might stress jobs that can be done conveniently within a busy or unpredictable schedule, even at home, and which have a short, fixed time commitment.

By examining and interviewing your current volunteer population you should get a good start in developing a list of targets. But you should be careful not to assume that this list will represent all of the potential groups who might be interested in the job. Once you have developed a list of the characteristics of the volunteers who have enjoyed the job, start thinking about

---

PROMPT QUESTIONS
'Who would want to do the job?'

◆ Who currently does it?

◆ What jobs or occupations do they have?

◆ Who once did it and has now left or retired?

◆ Who would like to be doing it, but is now in a job where it is not possible? Who was educated to do this, but now has a different type of job?

◆ Who could learn to do it?

◆ Who is now learning to do it and intends to do it more in the future? What schools or colleges teach this subject?

◆ Who can get someone else who is qualified to do it? Can you find a teacher or a senior practitioner in this skill who can recommend and encourage others in their field to help you?

◆ Who has a radically different job, such that this would be an exciting novelty?

---

what other types of people are likely to have similar backgrounds or interests, and try to expand the list of potential targets before you begin analysing how to locate and approach each potential target group.

Targeted recruitment tends to work best when you are looking for a particular type of skill, such as experience in accounting. It tends to work somewhat with psychological characteristics, but only if they are sufficiently identifiable (such as a love for children or a liking for sports).

Where will you find them?

If you are after a certain type of professional, there are often professional societies or clubs where such people might be found. If you are after members of a given age group or a certain ethnic group, try to identify those places where such people gather. Where do they shop? Where do they worship? Where do they go for recreational activity? Again, if you simply begin trying to recruit anyone in the general community, the answer to these questions is 'everywhere'. This will make your job more difficult because it will be harder to focus your recruitment effort. People who are everywhere are also nowhere in particular.

The answer to the question 'Where will you find them?' will inevitably affect the recruitment methods that can be used. For example, if you are trying to recruit young professionals you might put an advertisement in a glossy magazine. If you are recruiting teenagers with time on their hands, you might distribute leaflets outside school or give a talk to the local sixth form college. Several volunteer programmes have recruited single people by advertising in singles bars. If the potential volunteers live in a particular neighbourhood, you might go door-to-door (a technique often used by neighbourhood and community associations).

The answer might also lead you to speak to certain groups. Such groups might be formal or informal, and your talk to them might be a prepared speech or a casual conversation. Communities tend to be made up of circles of people – social groups, groups of employees, clubs, professional organisations, and so on. In identifying who you are after and where they are to be found, you move toward identifying the circles of people you want to reach in order to present your recruitment message.

People also belong to readership, listening, and viewing groups. If you are going to use the media in your campaign, you need to select which media to use based on the profile of its listeners/ viewers/readers. Any newspaper, radio, or television station can supply you with such information.

How should you go about communicating with them?

This step is implied by the previous one, and if you have done a good job of figuring out where they can be reached, developing an appropriate message is easy.

In general, the most effective methods of volunteer recruitment are those in which two-way communication is possible. The best form is communication from a current volunteer or board member, since they are attributed with purer motives than those of paid staff. There is always the subconscious suspicion that the paid person is trying to get the potential volunteer to do some of the work that they do not want to do.

One of the weaknesses of having no particular target group in mind is that it is difficult to use methods that involve two-way communication. If you are trying to recruit members of the general community who are everywhere you have to fall back on one-way communication such as direct mail, press releases, posters, newspaper ads, or flyers. Such efforts do succeed in recruiting volunteers, but they are less efficient in recruiting effective, dedicated volunteers than those methods in which a potential volunteer can ask questions and where you can address the candidate's own needs and skills.

People volunteer only because they want to. Helping a person see that they can do something they want to do is easiest when a two-way conversation can take place. Therefore, while you should include easy and inexpensive methods of recruiting volunteers in any recruitment drive, you will be most effective if you put an emphasis on one-to-one conversations and on talking to groups small enough to get a good two-way conversation going.

Recruiting through such methods is more labour-intensive than a one-way communication campaign which may mean involving other people in the recruitment process. It means the volunteer coordinator needs to manage the recruiting effort, not do it all themselves.

What are the motivational needs of these people?

It is important that the recruitment message speak directly to the motivational needs of the potential volunteer. If, for example, you are going to target newcomers to town, you might surmise that one of their motivational needs would be to make new friends. You would then make sure that your recruitment campaign includes the fact that the volunteer will meet lots of friendly, interesting people while they do the valuable work you are asking of them.

When you identify your target groups, you can then guess at which other needs might be important to individuals in that group. You can then send a message which speaks directly to those needs. People might respond to messages stressing motivators as diverse as patriotism, a need to protect their families, or a need to advance their careers.

Shown overleaf is a very effective ad designed to recruit macho males. It speaks effectively to a person who needs to feel tough, and who needs

Possible motives for volunteering

- to get out of the house
- to get to know important people in the community
- to gain new skills which might improve employment prospects
- to make a transition from prison, mental illness or similar situations to the real world
- to test the waters before making a career change
- to make new friends
- to be with old friends who are already volunteering at the organisation
- to gain knowledge about the problems of the community
- to maintain skills they no longer use otherwise
- to impress their present employer
- to spend quality time with members of their family by volunteering together
- to gain status
- to escape boredom
- to feel part of a group
- to express a religious or philosophical belief
- to exercise skills in a different context

MEN WANTED
for hazardous journey

Small wages, bitter cold, long months of complete darkness, constant danger, safe return doubtful. Honour and recognition in case of success.

to test himself in very demanding physical circumstances. It was used by Scott and Shackelton for their Antarctic expedition. A similar appeal was used successfully by a volunteer director who had been having a very difficult time trying to find people to escort children to school through gangland housing estates.

What will you say to them?

Often no thought is given to the message at all – you just send people out to talk about what the organisation does and about the kinds of volunteer jobs you want people to do. By doing this, you needlessly reduce the number of people who will respond to you. An effective recruitment message has four parts.

The need

The statement of need tells the volunteer why the job they will be doing is important. Most recruitment messages seldom talk about why you want the person to do a particular job. They only talk about the activities the person will be performing. This leaves it up to the person being recruited to figure out what the need for those activities is. The need usually refers to something that exists in the community, not something that exists inside the organisation. 'Our OAP centre needs volunteers to help cook hot meals for pensioners one day a week' is not the kind of statement we are referring to. The problem with such a statement is that it conjures up the picture of sweating over a hot stove, and there are few people who are likely to be excited about doing that. Many, however, would find their interest engaged by the opportunity to do something to 'enhance the lives of the elderly'. By including this kind of statement of need in the recruitment message, you show people how they can help solve a problem rather than merely undertake an activity.

PEOPLE ARE HUNGRY

Somebody should do something about that.

BE SOMEBODY.

Call [the organisation].

A very powerful and simple recruitment message

Statements naturally lead the potential volunteer to think 'That's terrible; somebody should do something about that'. Once the person is thinking this way, it is a simple step to recognising that they could be that person. Recruiting them then becomes easy.

> ## The need
>
> Often, for volunteers involved in providing a direct service, the need will be that of the clients to be served. A few such statements of need are listed below.
>
> ◆ **Hospital Volunteer:** 'Many patients in the hospital for long stays are lonely and depressed.'
>
> ◆ **Crisis Volunteer:** 'Some people in our community suffer from mental fear and anguish so intense that they do harm to themselves and to other people.'
>
> ◆ **Literacy Volunteer:** 'Many people from all walks of life are unable to take advantage of the full benefits of our society because they are unable to read or write.'
>
> ◆ **Girl Guide Leader:** 'Many girls grow up without the self-confidence and other skills to become competent, successful adults.'
>
> ◆ **Mental Health Centre Receptionist:** 'Clients coming into the centre are often embarrassed, confused, and uneasy.'
>
> ◆ **Museum Guide:** 'Many people who will visit the museum would like to know more about the exhibits. Sometimes their lack of knowledge causes them to miss a great deal of the meaning and beauty of the exhibits, and their interest in returning to the museum wanes.'
>
> ◆ **Carer:** 'Some senior citizens live in housing developments with little or no contact with other people or the outside world. They are sometimes sick, in need of assistance, or even dying, and no one is aware of their plight.'

In responding to statements of need, the volunteer is directly answering the needs that the organisation itself exists to address. On the other hand, some volunteers are recruited to do things that do not directly affect the organisation's main work. Some clerical volunteer jobs, for example, exist to meet the needs of staff or of the organisation more than they do the needs of clients or the community.

In talking about the need in such circumstances, it is important to talk about the needs of the staff in the context of their work in meeting the needs of the community. A few examples of what you might say are listed below.

◆ **Voluntary Action Centre Secretary/Typist:** 'When people call wondering what they can do to help make the community a better place, staff are sometimes limited in their responses because the information they have is not filed systematically and not typed.'

◆ **Community Action Organisation Bookkeeper:** 'In order to continue our efforts to improve the lives of the poor, we must account for our grants properly, a skill none of our staff have.'

The statement of need should lead the potential volunteer naturally to the conclusion that something ought to be done about it. In one-to-one or small group situations, the recruiter can stop at this point to check to see if the potential volunteers agree that this is a need worth doing something about. Often, in such situations, the potential volunteer may stop to remark on the seriousness of the situation. Once you get a volunteer thinking that somebody should do something about the problem, recruitment is as easy as showing them that they could be that person.

Returning to the example of the old people's centre, the recruiter might ask the potential volunteer if they were aware that many senior citizens in the community were unable to afford nutritionally balanced meals and were suffering from malnutrition. The recruiter might include some anecdotal evidence or some statistics, though these are often less compelling in conversation than stories about actual people. If the volunteer doesn't say anything, the recruiter might ask what they think about it.

The job
All this then leads naturally to the second element of an effective recruitment message, which is to show the volunteer how he or she can help solve the problem. In other words, now is the time to talk about the job you want the volunteer to do. By describing these activities in the context of the need, you make your recruitment message more powerful. If you merely jump in and talk about the activities without defining the need, not everyone will be able to figure out why such activities are important. By making the assumption that people will automatically see why the work is worth doing, you needlessly screen out people who would like to give their time to a worthwhile effort, but aren't able to see immediately why this job is important. Using our example, the potential volunteer might be quite eager to help out in the kitchen to help overcome the problem of malnutrition, while she may be totally uninterested in the job if it is merely described as cooking, washing dishes, or serving meals.

When talking to a potential volunteer about a job, the recruiter should attempt to help the volunteer see themself doing the job. You need to make your description of the job as vivid as possible. Talk about the physical environment, the people they will meet, and all the minor details that create a full image of the situation the volunteer will encounter.

The picture you create should stress the positive elements of the job in order to encourage the person to volunteer, but it should also be honest. Although recruiting does have something in common with selling a product, you must not glamourise or misrepresent the job. If you are trying to sell a product, you might exaggerate the positive aspects of it, but in recruiting you are trying to show a volunteer that they can do something they want to do. If they volunteer under false pretences, you will probably waste time training and trying to motivate a person who will not last long in the job.

In addition to painting a picture of the job to be done, you want to put the volunteer in the picture. A good technique to use in this regard is to ask the person some questions about how they would react in certain job situations. These situations should be easy and pleasant ones to handle, not questions such as 'What will you do if a client throws up on you?'.

The questions should assume that the person is indeed going to volunteer. Avoid saying 'If you decide to do this'. Instead, ask questions such as:

◆ What hours will be best for you?

◆ What appeals to you most about this work?

◆ What can you do to make the experience fun for yourself?

◆ Will you be able to attend our staff meetings?

Fears

For some situations, it will be necessary to address potential fears that a volunteer might have. The best way to deal with such issues is to be straightforward, reassuring the volunteer that the organisation recognises the problem and then letting the volunteer know what steps the organisation has taken to help counter the problem. Steps could include providing extensive training for the volunteer, conducting an orientation in how to protect oneself against infection, or providing regular health checks, and so on.

Most volunteers are more afraid of the unknown than of any recognised risk. This means that potential problems are less likely to deter them from volunteering if they are addressed openly, and if the organisation seems to be responsible in dealing with them.

Fears might include:
◆ a client that is viewed as dangerous
◆ a type of work at which the volunteer has little experience
◆ a part of town that is unfamiliar to the volunteer
◆ a disease that is viewed as potentially dangerous or infectious to the volunteer.

Often the easiest way to address these fears is during a one-to-one discussion with a volunteer, but they can also be addressed

VOLUNTEER COUNSELLORS NEEDED

The Fairfax Victim Assistance Network is accepting applications from volunteers to join a dedicated team who counsel victims of domestic violence and sexual assault.

Extensive training will be provided on counselling skills, crisis intervention, advocacy and community resources.

Persons with diverse backgrounds and life experiences are encouraged to apply.

Call xxx-xxxx for info and application.

in other formats, as the newspaper advertisement *(left)* shows. The advertisement addresses two potential fears. The first is a lack of qualification for the task of counselling, which is met in the sentence offering 'extensive training' . The other fear is that the job is only being offered to professionals, which is countered in the penultimate sentence.

Benefits

In addition to talking about the need and the job, the message should also talk about the potential benefits to be gained from the job. This fourth part of the message helps people see how they can help themselves by doing activities that help an organisation serve the community.

To be as effective as possible, the recruitment message needs to show the potential volunteer that whatever combination of needs they have can be met by the organisation. This section of the message is particularly important in recruiting volunteers for clerical or staff support jobs, such as the legendary envelope stuffer. People don't volunteer to stuff envelopes because of the job or for the satisfaction of creating mountains of mail. They do it other reasons, the most common being the pleasure of socialising with a group of other people while they do this important, if not very exciting task.

If the recruitment message is presented in a one-way format, it should list some of the benefits which the volunteer coordinator thinks will appeal to the target group. If it is being presented in two-way format, where the recruiter has an opportunity to talk to potential volunteers about their needs, skills, and desires, the benefits can be tailored specifically to the audience.

Because each volunteer has different motivations for volunteering, the recruiter needs to know something about the intending volunteer in order to do the most effective job of encouraging her to volunteer. If the person wants to gain work experience, you should propose jobs that allow them to do that.

If the recruiter doesn't know the person they are trying to recruit, and if the circumstances allow, they should spend some time with the person to find out what kinds of benefits might appeal.

This situation also provides the opportunity to identify some things the potential volunteer is concerned about and enjoys doing, and other clues to what it is they want to do. This may lead to the development of new volunteer opportunities.

A person who wants to help might have an active interest in photography. As the recruiter talks to the person about helping out in the kitchen (which is what the organisation wants them to do), they may notice that the volunteer is only mildly interested. When they talk about photography, however, interest perks up. The recruiter might then ask if the volunteer would be interested in using their photographic skills to help the organisation.

If the recruiter learns what kinds of benefits are important to the volunteer, it is important that these be communicated to the volunteer coordinator so that they can make sure the volunteer's needs are met. One cause of high volunteer turnover is that volunteers don't get the tasks they volunteered to do. They might have volunteered to be with particular friends and were assigned to different shifts; they might have volunteered to get involved in a regular, soothing, non-stressful activity and were given a high-risk task; they might have volunteered to learn new skills and didn't get the chance to do anything beyond what they already know; or they volunteered to impress their employer and didn't get a letter of thanks sent to their boss, and so on. The information obtained from effective recruiting is the same information that can be used in successful volunteer retention.

> **CHILDREN ARE BEING ABUSED**
>
> **You can help by offering temporary shelter.**
>
> **We'll show you how you can help these children and help yourself at the same time.**
>
> Call (phone number).

Even if space is limited, include all these elements in your message. Here, for example, is a four sentence recruitment message that fits on a poster.

The statement of benefits in the recruitment message, like the statement of need, is often left out by recruiters – perhaps because they ascribe purer motives to volunteers or because it is so obvious to them. Leaving this out, however, needlessly reduces the number of people you can attract to assist your organisation.

Stating the need, the job, the negating of fears, and stressing the benefits are all essential if you are to have the best chance of recruiting as many effective people as possible. Regardless of the types of recruitment methods you use, tell the people what the problem is (show the need); show them how they can help solve it (describe the job); alleviate their concerns (deal with fears); and tell them what they will gain (indicate the benefits) in the process.

Who will do the recruiting?

This is the time to decide how to get more two-way communication into the recruiting effort and who will take the responsibility for creating posters, contacting radio stations, and other forms of one-way communication.

An often overlooked and extremely effective resource is a volunteer who is taken on specifically to recruit other volunteers. If you are looking for volunteers from the workplace, for example, an effective first step is to recruit an employee whose volunteer job is to identify other potential volunteers within the company and recruit them for jobs that they want to do. Such a person can play this role year-round, thus providing more flexibility for other means of recruitment. Every time a need for a volunteer arises, the volunteer coordinator can put the word out through the volunteer recruiters. These people can then approach others they know who might be interested in the new volunteer opportunity.

An effective volunteer programme might have volunteer recruiters in a variety of different groups in the community. Such a network, once established, enables the volunteer coordinator to use the most effective form of recruitment – face-to-face contact with someone you know – in a systematic and easy way. A good way of setting up such a system is to have staff, committee members, and other volunteers think about people they know in the various community groups who might be willing to volunteer their time. These people can then be brought together for a training session.

How will they know what to do?

The last step in preparing the recruitment effort is to train those who will be delivering the recruitment message. If you follow the principles described above, this means training everyone involved with the organisation. Everybody knows potential volunteers; it's just a matter of getting them to think about asking those people to make a commitment to an organisation and of equipping them to make a coherent case for so doing.

In general, training should cover the participant's role in the recruitment process and provide adequate opportunity for them to role-play their presentation of the recruitment message. Ways to make sure participants learn from the training experience are covered in the chapter on training.

"The most effective people to be involved in recruitment are often those who are volunteers or management committee members of the organisation. In order to ensure their effectiveness, however, you need to be sure they know this is their responsibility, who they are supposed to recruit, where to find those people, how they are supposed to do it, and what they are supposed to say. In short, they need to be well prepared by the volunteer coordinator to do the most effective job possible."

Combining targeting and warm body recruitment

By carefully wording your mass media communication you can actually make use of targeted recruitment.

By using targeted recruitment techniques to identify the motivations of likely volunteers you can design a mass media campaign which will generate a greater number of qualified and interested applicants.

Concentric circle recruitment

Concentric circle recruitment is the lazy way to always have a flow of replacement volunteers applying to work at your organisation. It works through the simple theory that those people who are already connected to you and your organisation are the best targets for a recruitment campaign.

First, attempt to locate a volunteer for the position by starting with the groups of people who are already connected to you and then work outwards. You might capitalise on the fact that most volunteers are recruited by those people who they already know. You could ask the recumbent in a job to ask a friend to volunteer to replace them. You might look among former clients or your current volunteers for a replacement. This approach will make it easier to get a positive response, because the group of potential volunteers will already be favourably disposed toward your organisation. Similar techniques are

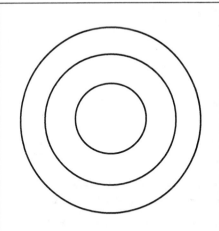

To visualise the theory of concentric circles, simply think of ripples in a pond when a rock is thrown in. Starting in the centre of contact, the ripples spread outwards. Concentric circles volunteer recruitment operates in the same manner.

used in fundraising (donor get a donor) and in membership drives, (member get a member). They are simple, effective, and cost effective.

'Who asked you to volunteer?'	
	%
Friend	52.0
Someone at church or synagogue	28.3
Family member or relative	25.0
My employer	7.9
Organisation representative	7.9
Teacher/school activities leader	4.0
Other	5.1
Don't know	1.8

1990 Gallup Poll — Independent Sector

These results *(left)* indicate one of the simple reasons for the remarkable success of concentric circles recruitment. Since it often involves face-to-face recruitment by those who already know the people whom they are approaching, one of its strengths is the personal testimony of the volunteer. During the conversation, the volunteer can say, either directly or indirectly, 'This is a good volunteer job with a good organisation. I know this because I worked there and I think it is worth your time to work there too'. This is a very credible and persuasive argument that mass media techniques and appeals from complete strangers have a hard time equalling.

Ideal groups around whom to structure your concentric circles recruitment include:

♦ Current volunteers
♦ Friends and relatives of volunteers
♦ Clients
♦ Friends and relatives of clients
♦ 'Alumni' (clients and volunteers)
♦ Staff
♦ Donors
♦ People in the neighbourhood
♦ Retired people in your field or subject

Even more direct evidence of the efficacy of concentric circles recruitment was seen in a result of the 1987 Gallup Survey, also available from Independent Sector: among those who have been recipients of services by a community organisation, 23% volunteer; among non-recipients, only 9% volunteer. The service received need not have been given directly by the soliciting organisation, but may instead be of a similar type to that received by those being asked to volunteer. One campaign to recruit volunteers for the alcoholism treatment unit in a hospital consisted of letters to members of a local Alcoholics Anonymous group. Each letter was jointly signed by the volunteer coordinator of the hospital and by a current member of the AA group (thus tapping two elements of the concentric circle concept).

These examples demonstrate that a clear strength of the concentric circles theory is that it concentrates on approaching those who may already have a good reason for helping out, either because they have received services themselves or they have seen the impact of the services on others. They have thus become convinced both of the need for the services and of the ability of your organisation to assist those with that need; all that remains is to demonstrate to them that they are capable of helping in meeting that need.

In short, any group which has already been favourably exposed to your programme makes an excellent target for a concentric circles recruitment campaign. All you need to do to capitalise on this receptivity is to start a word of mouth recruitment campaign and a constant trickle of potential volunteers will approach your organisation. Continually stress to all of these groups that they are essential to your recruitment campaign, and help them in knowing the types of volunteers you are looking for and the ways in which they can assist in finding and recruiting those volunteers.

Although a lot of effective person-to-person recruiting just happens, you can make a lot more of it happen by systematically encouraging it. Everyone involved in the organisation, both volunteers and staff, should understand what their recruitment responsibilities are within the framework of the overall plan. Each time a need for a new volunteer arises, the volunteer coordinator prepares a job description, and a rough statement of the need and possible benefits. This can be communicated to all staff, committee members, and current volunteers (especially those recruited for this purpose) so that they might begin looking, among the people they know, for good candidates.

If you are a new organisation you will probably not be able to take advantage of concentric circles recruitment, and will have to rely on the less effective methods of mass media and targeting. In time, however, you will build up goodwill among sufficient groups of people to take advantage of this simplest and most efficient method of recruitment.

Recruiting for difficult situations

Recruiting for a controversial cause, for a job perceived as dangerous, or for one that is recognised as difficult, is obviously harder than for easy jobs. Recruitment can be particularly difficult when the nature of the cause or the job is likely to provoke an initial fear reaction from the potential volunteer. The following are some suggestions for designing a recruitment campaign for these types of volunteer positions.

- Do advertise via local TV, radio, or newspapers so that thousands of potentially recruitable people see the message. In essence, saturate the community with your recruitment message. Some of the people you reach won't be afraid.

- Solicit those who are acquainted with the problem area because they already work with it, or are in an industry related to it, and thus do not have the same level of fear as the general public. Be sure to remember ancillary and connected industries, such as educators who teach in subject areas that discuss the problem area. You can also solicit the families of those who work in the subject area.

- Ask those who once worked with the problem area or those who are seeking careers related to the cause.

- Solicit former clients, their families, and their friends and relatives. This group is less likely to be afraid, more likely to identify with your group because they have received services, and quite likely to be committed to doing something about the problem.

- Recruit via current volunteers. Emphasise word of mouth communication. Their personal communication skill ('I work in this area and I know that it is both safe and rewarding') will often overcome barriers to involvement.

- Start with recruiting people for a non-controversial job in your organisation. Develop a two-tier recruitment system. First recruit them for a safe and easy job, then offer them a tough assignment after they've got to know you better.

- Create an educational programme to combat the fear. Start offering seminars in the community giving the true facts about the situation. Use some of your more motivated volunteers as spokespeople talking about their experiences. Recruit from those who attend the seminars.

- Use the targeted recruitment approach, identifying people who would want to do the job. A dangerous job might appeal to certain types of people.

- Bring people to you for some completely different reason (The London Lighthouse, for example, organises evening concerts). This gives visitors a chance to come to your premises, perhaps feel warm about your organisation, and pick up a bit of literature.

Combining alternative job design with recruitment efforts

It is also possible to enhance your recruitment effort by trying variations in volunteer job design. These variations may be considered where difficulties are encountered in finding adequate numbers of volunteers because of the complexity of the volunteer position.

One way to approach difficult recruitment is to make the 'volunteer' not one person, but several. If the difficulty is that the job is too large for a single individual, then the obvious solution is to make it the responsibility of more than one person. You can approach this via two different methods.

1. Volunteer job sharing

The classic job-sharing approach is to make the volunteer unit a partnership, with two people sharing the job, or make the job one done by a lead volunteer who is given an assistant. The two people can split up the time and work requirements. This approach is particularly useful when you are trying to encourage a volunteer who has a particular expertise, but is reluctant to volunteer because they don't feel they have the time to do all of the work. Here, a volunteer assistant can provide the hands; the expert volunteer can provide the brains.

An interesting advantage of job sharing is that it benefits all parties. It will enable you to induce reluctant volunteers to attempt new challenges and to convince tired volunteers to remain on a bit longer. A properly constructed partnership may be synergistic, resulting in a whole that is stronger than the sum of its parts. Team members may individually lack skills which are compensated for by others, resulting in a more effective working group than any one individual can be.

The disadvantages of job sharing are twofold. First, it requires careful matching of the personalities who will be involved. They must be compatible in personality, vision of the job, and work style to successfully form a team. Second, it requires greater management and supervision, particularly during its early stages when the partnership is developing relationships and working arrangements. If you assign volunteers to work together, schedule a review session for about a month after the volunteers have been matched. Turn this session into a discussion of their working relationship, using it to determine whether they have made the transition to a smooth working unit, and whether their personalities are suitable for a situation of shared responsibility.

While the word 'team' describes this type of job-sharing relationship, it is important to note that the team should not include more than two people. Job-sharing with three or more people is nearly impossible to accomplish without a lot of work. Larger groups begin to function more as committees, and the nature of that larger social interaction can result in factions and alliances.

2. Group volunteering

Recruit an entire group as the volunteer unit. The group might include an entire family, a club, or even a business. The group sub-divides the work, lessening the time burden on any single member. Start this process by recruiting one member of the group who will persuade the others to become involved, making the volunteer job their project.

Both of these approaches are substantiated by data from the US where a study showed that 71% of non-volunteers said they would be attracted by a volunteer opportunity in which they could work with friends or peers, and 55% said they would be interested in an opportunity to do volunteer work with their families. By giving them these opportunities, you are essentially creating positions in which the volunteer can simultaneously do good and spend time with others.

A demonstration project on family volunteering conducted by VOLUNTEER: The National Centre suggested the following characteristics for design of successful family volunteer jobs:

- The time commitment is flexible, often beginning with one-shot or short-term jobs that have the potential to grow into continuing activities.

- The jobs have understandable goals and logical, specific activities to be undertaken.

- The jobs provide something relevant for every member of the family.

- The jobs take advantage of the unique nature of family relationships.

- The jobs provide an opportunity to work with other volunteers, particularly other families.

Your search for volunteer groups may lead you into some strange places. Consider, for example, *Lifers Group, Inc*, a volunteer club that operates out of East Jersey State Prison in the US. The convicts have established a group that helps local organisations raise money and other resources. Or the high school students in Philadelphia who have formed a group to provide volunteer computer assistance to local organisations and other students. They call the programme 'Dial-a-Nerd'.

Management of these volunteer groups will depend on an existing natural leader as your key supervisory mechanism. The group must enforce its own rules, and will resist too much direct outside intervention. Make sure that you have worked out a way of relating to the group leader, and use them to train and direct the group.

Groups often rotate leadership, as does Doing Something, a volunteer group for young professionals in Washington, DC: *'Volunteers are encouraged to take the lead on a project that interests them and to coordinate the activities of the project. By rotating responsibilities, the group avoids letting one volunteer take on too much, and acts as a safeguard against burnout'.*

Ease them in

One of the reasons for saying no to a high-time or high-involvement position is that the volunteer is afraid. This fear might be based on a feeling that the volunteer won't like the job enough to devote the time and energy to it, or that it isn't worth the investment which it requires on the part of the volunteer. It might equally be based on a fear that the volunteer won't be able to do the job well enough, and a reluctance to let the organisation down.

All of these difficulties can be dealt with by introducing the volunteer to the position gradually rather than expecting them to buy the whole package at once. Here are some ways to let the volunteer become accustomed to the more difficult position.

Test driving

Offer the potential volunteer a trial period (of 30 days, for example). Tell them to try the job and see if they like it enough to keep it. This is a great approach because it allows the volunteer to see if they like the job and the organisation to see if they like the volunteer.

Schedule a review meeting when the volunteer starts the position and stress that the volunteer is under no obligation to continue the job after the trial period. While you will lose some volunteers, you will gain quite a few who have had the opportunity to try the job without pressure, learned that they liked the work, and decided that investing their time and energy is worth it.

The implicit promise to the volunteer is 'Try it, you'll like it!'. And the reassurance is that the volunteer can honourably withdraw if they don't feel as though they really want to do the job. At that point, however, the resourceful volunteer coordinator will try to negotiate another job for them with the organisation – a smart move in this case, since anyone can persuade someone to volunteer once, the trick is to find them a job they will stick with and enjoy.

Apprenticeships

Apprenticeships work by making the volunteer an aide to the person who currently does the job. The volunteer then operates as an assistant at the direction of this volunteer.

Apprenticeships work exceptionally well for leadership jobs or jobs with large amounts of responsibility which people are reluctant to take because they don't feel totally comfortable about being able to do the work well. Examples of good positions for considering apprenticeships are chairs of committees or special events, or technical jobs which require decision-making experience which the volunteer does not currently possess.

During the apprenticeship they can learn to do the work until they are comfortable with their ability to handle it well. When the person in the job moves on the apprentice is then ready for promotion into a position which they will now think they have earned and for which they are prepared.

A variation on apprenticeship is the mentor or buddy system. In these cases, the senior volunteer does not directly supervise the new volunteer but serves to provide advice as requested or needed, and often will operate as a coach to the newcomer.

Propinquity

This method works through obtaining a volunteer for a difficult position by first recruiting them for something else instead. Propinquity is the process of becoming accustomed to and favourably disposed toward those things or people which you are around and used to.

Things, people, or jobs which seemed too large, too difficult or too frightening because they are new or strange may no longer seem quite so daunting after the volunteer has been around them for a while.

In propinquity recruitment, you attempt to recruit a person for another position which is near or connected to the position for which you eventually want them to serve.

For example, if your organisation was having trouble recruiting counsellors for one-to-one work with emotionally disturbed children, you might recruit someone to assist in collecting data from the volunteers currently doing that job. Data collection is a small and simple job that is easily done, but while doing it the volunteer is exposed to the more difficult job and can learn to understand it and how valuable it is. Through the process of propinquity, data collection volunteers are more likely to become attached to the counselling job with which they are in contact. When then asked to consider becoming counsellors they are likely to be more willing because the position is familiar to them.

One way to view recruitment by propinquity is that you are simply creating a new population of concentric circle volunteers who will become interested in the job. Any way that you view it, it works: people are much less reluctant to take jobs that they understand and are accustomed to. In recruitment by propinquity, the job ends up speaking for itself.

IDENTIFYING POTENTIAL RECRUITMENT APPEALS

All of the above methods for volunteer recruitment require the recruiter to develop a message explaining what the organisation is offering to the volunteer, and which will tap into some motivational impulse of that volunteer. The possible range of volunteer motivations is very broad, and this tends to lead organisations to develop very broad motivational appeals, in the belief that someone amongst all those potential volunteers will respond. However, it is important to realise that what is needed in the recruitment appeal is a slightly narrower approach, motivating potential volunteers not just to decide to volunteer, but to volunteer with this particular organisation, doing this particular job.

The appeal can then focus on communicating to the potential volunteer why the organisation and its work are important, and how the potential volunteer could contribute to the accomplishment of that work. Different aspects of this message may be stressed more than others, or may be communicated differently in different recruitment drives. An appeal to young people, for example, might stress work

---

Recruitment appeals

To create a more defined appeal, you should develop answers to four key questions which can be communicated to potential volunteers

◆ **Why should this volunteer job be done?**
What is the need in the community for this work? What will happen if this job is not done?

◆ **What will the benefit be to the community or to the clients?**
What will the work accomplish? What changes will it make in people's lives?

◆ **What are some possible fears or objections concerning this job which must be overcome?**
The type of clients? The subject area? The skills needed to do the work? Geography?

◆ **What will be the personal benefit to the volunteer in doing the job?**
Skills? Experience? Flexible work schedules? New friends?

experience possibilities, while an appeal to previous clients of the organisation may talk about the effects of the problem and the ability to help others obtain the support that they themselves have experienced.

Creating an effective message is much more difficult than it seems, particularly when this is being done by paid employees. Quite often their own extensive knowledge of the organisation and its work interferes with writing an effective appeal; in a sense they are too familiar with the subject to remember that others lack that basic knowledge. They will often forget to include the most basic of facts – number of people in the community who face the problem; harmful effects of the condition – because they assume that others in the community are as familiar with the situation as they are. Their own intimate relationship with the situation makes them think that others are equally aware. This means that field-testing recruitment appeals is quite important, to make sure that the general population receives the appropriate information in a way which they can both understand and relate to.

STARTING A RECRUITMENT CAMPAIGN

As this chapter indicates, there are many possible ways for a volunteer programme to recruit volunteers. The smart volunteer manager will pick and choose methods depending on the desired results.

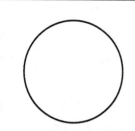

This circle represents the motivational needs of individuals that might be tapped in recruitment campaigns.

- A *warm body campaign* is good for when you need a large number of volunteers for an event, or when you are just beginning a programme and need to attract community attention.
- A *targeted recruitment campaign* is good for finding individuals with specific talents or interests.
- A *concentric circle campaign* is good for maintaining a steady flow of replacement volunteers.

Each type of campaign can successfully recruit volunteers; the trick is to select the campaign that will obtain the right types of volunteers with the least amount of effort.

Each campaign is dependent upon identifying the possible motivations that individuals might have and connecting these motivations to some volunteer opportunity that your organisation has to offer.

Suggestions for putting
an effective message into writing

1   The opening of the message is interesting enough to make the potential volunteer continue reading or listening.

2   The body of the message is appealing enough to the potential volunteer to make them consider the volunteer opportunity or, at least, to contact the organisation to get more information. Boring messages are only likely to appeal to boring people.

3   The body of the message presents information in an order that psychologically matches how people will think about the offer:

◆ **Need:** *Is there a problem?*

◆ **Solution:** *Can this job help solve it?*

◆ **Fears/Questions:** *Will I be capable of helping?*

◆ **Benefits:** *What's in it for me?*

◆ **Contact Point:** *How do I get involved?*

As a general rule, spend more space on need than on logistics. People will first decide whether you're worth volunteering for and then decide whether they can fit you into their schedule. The need you stress may be yours, your clientele's, or a perceived need/benefit for the volunteer.

4   The message is easily understood, intelligible and avoids jargon, unless it is included for a specific reason.

5   The message has been tested for ease of comprehension by someone other than the author of the message. Remember: *What can be misunderstood, will be.*

6   The message gives a complete picture: problem, type of work, requirements, timeframe, person to talk to. The message doesn't make the potential volunteer have to do any extra work in order to understand what is going on.

7   The contact information for the message gives the name of a person, preferably including their first name, not just the name of the organisation. Volunteering is a personal decision and people like to talk with other people about it.

CHAPTER SIX

Screening and Interviewing

One of the most neglected areas of volunteer management training has been that of effective interviewing of volunteers. This is unfortunate, since good interviewing skills are essential to performing that most crucial of all volunteer management tasks – matching a potential volunteer with a task and a working environment that they will enjoy. This chapter covers specific techniques as well as policies relevant to screening and interviewing volunteers.

Even more unfortunate is the fact that much of the management training which does exist on interviewing deals with employment interviewing, a totally inappropriate approach for volunteer interviewing. The main difference is quite easily stated: 'Volunteer interviewing consists of evaluating a person for *a* job, not for *the* job'. Effective volunteer interviewing does not so much consist of examining an applicant's suitability for one job as it does evaluating the ability and desire of that applicant to fit productively into some position within the organisation. Employment interviewing focuses on the question, 'Who can do this job?', while volunteer interviewing should focus on the more creative question, 'Who will want to do this job?'. Ivan Scheier called this 'the people approach' over twenty years ago, and that phrase still exemplifies the proper attitude to the process.

> **Topics covered include:**
>
> ◆ **Purposes of interviewing**
>
> ◆ **Organising the interview - interviewer and location**
>
> ◆ **Preparation for the interview**
>
> ◆ **The effective interview**
>
> ◆ **Matching the volunteers to jobs**

PURPOSES OF VOLUNTEER SCREENING

Among other things this difference in approach means that a volunteer interview has to accomplish more than the usual job interview. There are two basic purposes of a volunteer interview, described below.

Identify a fit

This includes determining the interests and abilities of the potential volunteer, determining their suitability for particular jobs, and assessing their appropriateness for the organisation; its style of operation, and its mission. 'Fit' is the interpersonal matching of the needs and interests of the volunteer with the needs and interests of the organisation. An examination of proper fit would include determining the following items regarding the volunteer.

◆ To what extent does the volunteer have both an interest in a particular job and the necessary qualifications to perform that job?

◆ To what extent does the volunteer have other interests and abilities that might be used to create a different job for them?

◆ To what extent is the volunteer suited for working in a particular job environment?

In many cases, suitability, which involves the likelihood that the volunteer will fit comfortably into the working environment, will be the key factor for success. Suitability could involve questions of personality (relaxed, frenetic; introverted, extroverted), style (neat, messy), behaviour (smoking, non-smoking), political philosophy (traditionalist, radical), or anything else which might affect how the volunteer will get along with the organisation in general, and with the particular staff group with whom they might be working. Very often these interpersonal relationship factors become more important than factors of technical qualification, which can be learned if the volunteer is willing to stay with the organisation. Quite simply, volunteers who are happy in their working environment will make the job happen; those who are unhappy will not.

Recruit

This includes answering any questions or concerns that the potential volunteer may have and persuading the volunteer of their ability to make a contribution to the organisation and its clientele, or that they will derive personal satisfaction from helping. It is a quite mistaken belief that the person who shows up for an interview has already decided to volunteer with the organisation.

During the process of the interview, it is crucial to remember that the volunteer has not yet been recruited. At this stage they have only been attracted to the organisation. One purpose of the interview is to give the volunteer an opportunity to look more closely at what the organisation has to offer, and for you to sell the organisation and its work to the volunteer. Equal time has to be given to focusing on why a particular job is important and interesting, as well as to whether the volunteer would be right for that job. Never assume that just because a volunteer has come to the interview, they are already a part of the organisation. If the screening interview is your first contact with the volunteer, then it is important that they feel welcomed and wanted during the interview process, and not as though they have already been caught by an uncaring bureaucracy which is only interested in determining which position the volunteer should fill.

INTERVIEWS

Choosing an interviewers

Since the time available for assessing potential candidates for volunteer positions is relatively short, it is important to have someone who is capable of making a satisfactory judgment conducting the interviews .

Volunteers often make better interviewers than paid staff, because they tend to be involved in fewer interviews and are therefore less likely to be burned out by the process. Conducting interviews is a draining process, and one which can easily be overwhelming. The common response in this situation is to stop listening after a while. Secondly, volunteers tend to be better able to build rapport with potential volunteers because, after all, they have something important in common – each thought the organisation was worth giving their time to.

Desirable abilities of a volunteer interviewer

- Broad knowledge of the organisation and its programmes
- Personal knowledge of staff and their individual personalities
- Ability to relate to all types of people
- Ability to talk easily with strangers
- Ability to listen attentively to what is said, and to perceive what is left unsaid
- Ability to ask follow-up questions
- Ability to follow the agenda of the interview without appearing to dominate
- Knowledge of non-directive interview techniques
- Ability to recruit and motivate while interviewing
- Commitment to the organisation and its programmes
- Ability to empathise with other people
- Ability to say 'no'

The location of the interview

Since a volunteer interview requires a greater exploration of personal characteristics, the choice of location can be critical. Three factors are important:

◆ accessibility

◆ a friendly atmosphere

◆ privacy.

The location for the interviewing process will vary, but it is important that the interviewee feel a sense of privacy and comfort. Do not conduct interviews in a public place or in a shared office, since this will deter many volunteers from offering full information about their backgrounds and interests.

Organise your own schedule so that you will not be interrupted during the interview, either by phone calls or by other staff. Besides disrupting the flow of the interview, interruptions give the volunteer the impression that they are much less important than your other work.

Remember the old adage: 'You never get a second chance to make a first impression'. What the potential volunteer sees and feels during the interview may shape their eventual attitude toward the organisation.

Pre-interview preparation

The following items should be prepared and ready before the interview:

◆ a list of volunteer jobs available, with descriptions of work and qualifications required;

◆ a list of questions to be asked in relation to each job;

◆ an application form completed by the volunteer with background information about them and their interest in you;

◆ a set of open-ended questions to explore the motivations of the volunteer;

◆ information and materials on the organisation and its programmes.

Opening the interview

You should open the interview by making the applicant feel welcome. Express appreciation that they have shown an interest in your organisation and taken the time to attend. Explain what you would like to accomplish and how they fit into the process.

The key to beginning a successful interview is to start building rapport with the potential volunteer. It is crucial that the interview process belongs as much to the volunteer as it does to the organisation. Let them know that their decision about whether volunteering with you would be suitable is the intention of the discussion. Let them feel in charge. Give them relevant background information about the organisation and its work, and make sure that you explain at the beginning of the interview that they should feel free to ask questions and express any concerns at any point during the discussion. The interview should be a mutual information exchange. It is a negotiation, not an interrogation.

Conducting the interview

The major portion of the interview should be devoted to the points outlined below.

- An exploration of the applicant's interests, abilities, and personal situation. Determine why the applicant is considering volunteering and what types of work environment they prefer.

- A discussion of various job possibilities. Explain the purpose and work situation of the different volunteer job opportunities available and let the applicant consider them. Use this as an opportunity to let the applicant discuss how they would approach various jobs, which will tell you more about their attitudes, their intentions and their level of interest.

- A discussion of your requirements: time commitments, training requirements, paperwork, confidentiality rules, etc. Let the volunteer know what will be expected of them.

Examples of questions which can be used during the interview

- What can I tell you about our organisation?
- What attracted you to our organisation? What aspect of our work most motivates you to seek to volunteer here?
- What would you like to get out of volunteering here? What will make you feel like your volunteering has been successful?
- What have you enjoyed most or least about your previous volunteer work? About your paid employment?
- Describe your ideal supervisor. How do you prefer that supervisor to relate to you?
- Would you rather work on your own, with a group, or with a partner? Why?
- What skills do you think you have to contribute?
- How would you spend the day if you could go anywhere and do anything?
- Are there any types of clients that you would most prefer to work with? Or that you would not feel comfortable working with?
- What do you think is the most important thing we should be doing to help our clients and to fulfil our mission in the community?
- How do you think you would go about this volunteer assignment? Where would you start and what do you think are the most important considerations? Give examples and reasons.

◆ Remember that you are still 'recruiting' the volunteer at this stage, so do not forget to explain why each job is important to the interests of the organisation and the clientele.

◆ Look for personality indicators that will help you match this person to a situation where they will be happy. This can include items such as whether they smoke, desire for individual or group work, and other preferences.

One of the important skills in an interviewer is the ability to detect an unexpected talent in the volunteer and to construct a possible volunteer role for them on the spot. This requires a good understanding of the organisation and its programmes. If you make use of volunteers to conduct interviews (where they are very effective in building rapport and seeing things from the viewpoint of the potential volunteer) make sure they have a good background about the organisation and how its work is organised.

While it is important to evaluate different elements for different volunteer jobs, here are some general areas to watch for while interviewing:

◆ ease in answering questions about personal qualifications and background

◆ ability to communicate well

◆ level of enthusiasm and commitment

◆ general attitudes and emotional reactions

◆ types of questions asked about the organisation and the position on offer

◆ other interests or hobbies

◆ flexibility

◆ maturity and stability

◆ preference for a group or individual setting for volunteer work

◆ level of self-confidence

◆ any sense of a hidden agenda

◆ time pattern of previous work and volunteer experience

◆ reasons for coming to the interview

◆ preferences in type of work.

Closing the interview

The interview should be concluded either by making an offer of a position to the volunteer, or politely explaining that you have no suitable openings for them at this time. If you are offering a position, explain what will happen next: making background or reference checks, arranging a second interview, notification of your final decision in writing, scheduling a training or induction session, and so on. Explain the process, the timeframe, and what is expected of the volunteer at each stage. Remember to obtain the permission of the volunteer to conduct any reference or background checks.

Other interview considerations

Face-to-face or over the telephone?

Some organisations are simply not in a position to conduct interviews in person. This obviously makes the recruitment process a less personal situation, and inhibits both the ability of the organisation to evaluate the volunteer and the volunteer to assess the organisation. Generally speaking, it is more desirable to conduct face-to-face interviews for job situations which have the following attributes:

- the job requires a long time commitment and thus a high motivational level on the part of the volunteer;
- the job entails responsibility or requires a capacity or skill above the ordinary;
- the job is sensitive because of the nature of the work or the relationship with clients.

If you are unable to conduct an in-person interview for a job which involves any of these characteristics, you should try to schedule a review (after 30 days, for example) to see how the volunteer is performing and how they are feeling.

Reference checks

It is also important to check a potential volunteer's credentials. This is particularly important where the volunteer position

> **Overall interview suggestions**
> - Make sure the interview is not interrupted. This will make it much easier for the interviewer and the candidate to be comfortable.
> - Be an active listener. You need to understand the candidate, and that requires paying very close attention both to what they are saying and what they are not saying during the interview.
> - Answer any questions about the organisation and its work openly and honestly. This will demonstrate both your sincerity and your intelligence. You can't hide things from people who may later work with the organisation and will therefore find out anyway.
> - Don't promise anything if you are not sure of being able to make a placement.
> - Describe the volunteer position honestly. Do not hide undesirable aspects of the job in the hope that the volunteer won't mind discovering them after they've signed up.
> - Evaluate people on an individual basis. Don't assume they're like anyone else that you've ever met.

requires licensing or certification, or where it involves working with a clientele with diminished capacities. If you are going to check an applicants references, it is important to notify them and obtain their permission. One way to do so is by having them sign a permission document, such as that shown below.

Note that not all types of reference would need to be checked for each volunteer, but what needs to be checked relates to a particular volunteer position.

Sample permission document to be signed by volunteer

I hereby allow .... [name of organisation] to perform a check of my background, including:

◆ criminal record

◆ driving record

◆ past employment/volunteer history

◆ financial history

◆ educational/professional status

◆ personal references

◆ medical history

◆ other persons or sources as appropriate for the volunteer jobs in which I have expressed an interest.

I understand that I do not have to agree to this background check, but that refusal to do so may exclude me from consideration for some types of volunteer work.

I understand that information collected during this background check will be limited to that appropriate to determining my suitability for particular types of volunteer work and that all such information collected during the check will be kept confidential.

I hereby extend my permission to those individuals or organisations contacted for the purpose of this background check to give their full and honest evaluation of my suitability for the described volunteer work and such other information as they deem appropriate.

Signed:..

Involving staff in volunteer interviewing

It is crucial that the staff who have responsibility for overseeing the job which the volunteer will be performing have some involvement in the interviewing process. That involvement might take several forms:

Assisting in writing questions and scenarios for use during the interview

This is a vital function where staff are more familiar with the demands and requirements of a particular job than the volunteer coordinator.

Participating in the actual interview

While this is possible, it is not normally recommended. The difficulty this creates is that it limits the ability of the volunteer interviewer to negotiate with the potential volunteer about more than one job. Instead, we recommend that staff be involved in direct interviewing only during a second interview with potential volunteers, after preliminary ideas regarding placement have been made.

CONTRACTING

You may wish to consider entering into a contract with volunteers once the interviewing and matching process has been satisfactorily concluded. Contracting does not actually involve a formal legal document, as much as it does the signing by both the organisation and the volunteer of a listing of the mutual commitments and intentions they are entering into. The agreement might specify the work which the volunteer is agreeing to perform, the timeframe, and the benefits and support which the organisation agrees to provide the volunteer.

The purpose of the contract is to emphasise the seriousness of both the organisation and the volunteer in entering into a relationship, and is not intended to convey a sense of legal responsibility. Contracts work particularly well with young volunteers.

Recruiting, interviewing and selecting

The British Red Cross publishes the following guidelines as part of its Volunteering Policy. As well as advising volunteer management on recruitment and selection, it forms the basis of mutual hopes and expectations between the volunteer and the organisation by outlining the responsibilities of each to the other.

Attracting and selecting our volunteers

◆ Go out of the way to welcome anyone who wishes to volunteer. All advertising, information and personal contact with anyone interested in volunteering should reflect our need and desire to encourage more people to volunteer – from every part of the community.

◆ Give potential volunteers full information about the work of the Society to help them decide what time they want to give and what work they want to do. Everyone interested in volunteering is interviewed informally in person and given a 'welcome pack' for information and discussion. Once they agree to volunteer they receive training to familiarise them with the British Red Cross.

◆ Draw up and agree a job description for a task or set of tasks wherever possible. This sets out the key qualities or skills we need. Talking this through with a volunteer helps to agree the commitment they want to make and to match them to a job they will enjoy and do well. It also helps in planning for local needs and identifying what training or support will be useful.

◆ Recognise that potential, enthusiasm and willingness to be trained are often more useful than experience, knowledge or qualifications.

◆ Tell each volunteer exactly who is immediately responsible for supporting and co-ordinating their work. This might be a Group Leader, Centre Organiser, Volunteer Co-ordinator or another named person.

Our responsibilities to volunteers

◆ Enable volunteers to receive the right training, tools and clothing for the job.
◆ Make a time for volunteers to discuss their work, one-to-one or in a group.
◆ Take every opportunity to thank and encourage them.
◆ Enable volunteers to understand health and safety requirements.
◆ Enable volunteers to claim any expenses for their work with the society.
◆ Tell volunteers that there are grievance and disciplinary procedures which they can use to resolve problems.

◆ Create the opportunity for all volunteers to have confidential reviews from time to time with their immediate supervisor or volunteer co-ordinator. Reviews need not be very formal but they give volunteers a good chance to comment on their work or any training or support they need.

Volunteers rights and responsibilities

It is important that our volunteers know what to expect and what is expected of them.

What volunteers can expect from the British Red Cross

◆ Opportunities to serve the community regardless of their background.

◆ The satisfaction of knowing that what they do is of real worth and that they are recognised and valued by the Society – whether the task they take on is great or small, and whatever time they can give.

◆ The confidence to do the job because they can rely on consistent support and resources.

◆ Ready access to the challenging and exciting opportunities and training which the British Red Cross can offer them.

What the British Red Cross asks of its volunteers

◆ Accept and work within the Fundamental Principles of the International Red Cross and Red Crescent Movement and within the Society's rules.

◆ Make new people welcome, and work as a team with other volunteers and staff.

◆ Carry out the agreed tasks, upholding standards and quality of service.

◆ Attend any support, training or supervision sessions useful for their tasks or their development.

◆ To keep confidential any information about anyone receiving a service from the British Red Cross.

◆ Recognise that fundraising plays an important part in the work of the Society, in addition to the other tasks they may do.

◆ Support and follow the British Red Cross equal opportunities policy.

◆ Be aware they could be called on to help in an appropriate capacity in the event of a major incident or national emergency.

MATCHING VOLUNTEERS TO POSITIONS

Determining the correct job for a volunteer involves questions of both qualification and temperament. The volunteer must certainly be capable of doing or learning to do the job for which they are selected. But it is equally important that the volunteer fit into the work situation. This means that the volunteer must be satisfied with the job being offered, and view the job as providing desirable and fulfilling work. It means that the work setting (including the hours and location of the job) must also be acceptable to the volunteer. And finally it means that the staff or other volunteers with whom the volunteer will be working must also be suitable. This last factor may ultimately be decided by some relatively personal factors, such as compatibility or personality type, style of work, or even whether one person smokes and the other doesn't. The purpose of this matching operation is to identify areas of common interest and common satisfaction, as well as potential areas of friction or difficulty.

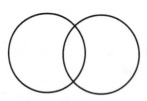

These circles represent the interests of the organisation and of the volunteer. The volunteer interview is designed to identify that area of overlap in which a volunteer job can be designed that satisfies both parties.

Since it is difficult to make totally accurate decisions in a 30-minute interview, it is desirable to offer all assignments on a trial-period basis. Let the volunteer know that the first 30 days of work will be done as a probationary period for both the volunteer and the organisation. At the end of this period, a second interview will be conducted in which both parties will re-evaluate the assignment. During this subsequent interview either party may request a change of assignment, based upon their additional knowledge of the situation.

This initial testing period will make it easier to encourage volunteers to try jobs about which they are uncertain and make it more likely that any problems will be identified early and corrected quickly.

CHAPTER SEVEN

Orientation and Training

Your volunteers are a valuable resource. Their time is a significant benefit to the organisation and helps the organisation achieve its goals. This chapter is about investing in your volunteers to improve their performance and enhance the contribution they make.

Every volunteer needs some level of induction before they begin working work with your organisation. This falls into three parts:

◆ orientation – the process of preparing the volunteer for a clear relationship with the organisation (sometimes known as induction);

◆ training – the process of preparing the volunteer to perform work for the organisation;

◆ coaching – the process of developing and upgrading skills.

Topics covered include:
◆ **Orienting the volunteers when they first arrive to the cause and the work, and to the structures and people of the organisation itself**
◆ **Providing the training they will need in information, skills, and approaches to the work**
◆ **Encouraging and facilitating volunteer learning on the job**
◆ **Providing future training opportunities as a volunteer benefit**

Every volunteer should know they will be required to attend an orientation and/or training session. Orientation is distinguished from training in that it is usually more general and informal, providing information every volunteer should know. Training is designed to equip volunteers with the specific skills and knowledge required by their position.

ORIENTATION

Even if volunteers come to the job with all the necessary skills, they will still need some orientation to the organisation. This will ensure that they feel comfortable with and understand the workings of the organisation. It is designed to provide them with background knowledge of the organisation and to let them understand how they can contribute to its aims. If the volunteer understands the organisation's systems, operations and procedures, they will be able to contribute more productively.

Cause orientation

This involves introducing the volunteer to the purpose of the organisation. It should cover:

◆ a description of the problem or cause;
◆ a description of the client group;
◆ a description of the mission and values of the organisation;
◆ a description of the history of the organisation;
◆ a description of the programmes and services of the organisation;
◆ a description of other groups working in the same field, and their distinguishing characteristics;
◆ a description of the future plans of the organisation.

> **There are three different subject areas which should be covered during the orientation process:**
> 1 The cause.
> 2 The systems for volunteer management.
> 3 The social environment for the volunteer.

The presentation of these items should be a discussion rather than a description. The intention of this part of the orientation is to allow the volunteer to learn and adopt the basic values of the organisation. Part of this may involve a debate over the philosophy and approach of the organisation; part may involve learning the history of the organisation through hearing stories about early leaders.

The goal of this discussion is to allow the volunteer to make an intellectual and emotional commitment to the basic purpose of the organisation, and to consciously decide that they believe in and are willing to work toward achieving the mission of the organisation.

System orientation

This involves introducing the volunteer to the system of volunteer management within the organisation. It may include a presentation and discussion of:

◆ the structure and programmes of the organisation, with illustrations of what volunteers contribute to those programmes;
◆ the system of volunteer involvement within the organisation; its policies and procedures;

- the facilities and equipment;
- volunteer requirements and benefits;
- record keeping requirements;
- the organisation's key activities and events and when they occur.

The simplest way to develop the agenda for this part of the orientation is to ask yourself 'What would I like to know about this place in order to better understand how it works?'. Remember that friends will ask the volunteers about their volunteer work and about the organisation. A volunteer who fully understands the organisation can serve as an effective communicator with the public about the worth of the organisation, while a confused volunteer can present quite the opposite.

The purpose of this part of the orientation is to provide an organisational context for the volunteer and make them understand how they fit into the organisation as a whole. This information is often presented in a factual way, with charts and descriptive handouts, followed by a question and answer period to clarify issues. It can be made more lively by having different representatives, both paid and volunteer, describe various aspects of the work of the organisation. The aim is to allow the volunteer to see how they will fit into helping address the need of the organisation, the basic requirements of their role, and how that role links to other areas of the organisation.

Social orientation

This part of the orientation introduces the volunteer to the social community which they are being asked to join and begins to forge the personal bonds that will sustain volunteer involvement.

Included in this are:

- an introduction to the leadership of the organisation (you must consider who could best present or lead part of the discussion on the mission of the organisation);
- a welcoming by staff and current volunteers (through their participation in presenting subject areas or even as a purely social occasion);
- a description of the culture and etiquette of the organisation (matters such as dress, customs, and so on).

This part of the orientation can proceed in a variety of ways. It might be interspersed throughout the other stages, with official greeting, welcoming, and presentation serving to initiate personal contacts. It might begin right after the formal acceptance of a volunteer, with the assignment of a personal mentor or companion who contacts the volunteers, meets with them informally to welcome them to the organisation and introduces them to its processes, and then supports them during their early involvement. It might consist of introducing the volunteer to their future supervisor and arranging for a discussion about how they will be working together. It might consist of a welcoming party for a new volunteer hosted by staff and current volunteers.

The purpose is to allow the volunteer to meet the people they will be working with, welcome them into the social context of the organisation, and show them that they are a welcome addition to the team.

The importance of orientation

Orientation is designed to answer three basic questions for the new volunteer

- ◆ Cause Orientation: *Why should I be working here?*
- ◆ System Orientation: *How will I be working here?*
- ◆ Social Orientation: *How do I fit in with everyone else?*

This information is crucial if the volunteer is to feel comfortable. A volunteer who does not feel right about these main aspects of volunteering will cease to feel a part of the organisation. Much of the early loss of volunteers in some organisations is due to the lack of a good orientation.

Some organisations avoid giving an orientation because of the difficulty in getting volunteers to attend. This might require altering the scheduling of orientations, holding them at weekends or during the evening, for example. It might involve altering the format of orientations, doing them one-on-one, in small groups, or in several shorter sessions. It may require making attendance mandatory, even if that means losing some potential volunteers. Make whatever adjustments are necessary, and ensure that all new volunteers receive a proper orientation.

Perhaps the best way of understanding the importance of orientation is to consider its basic definition. Orientation is the process of gaining one's direction and bearings in the world; a person without orientation is, to put it simply, lost.

TRAINING

Training is the process of providing volunteers with the ability to perform specific types of work.

Design of Training

Determining what training a volunteer may need requires answering three questions:

◆ what *information* do they need to successfully perform the work?

◆ what *skills* do they need to successfully perform the work?

◆ what *attitudes* or *approaches* do they need to successfully perform the work?

Training to provide this information, develop these skills and engender these attitudes can be provided in three formats: formal training sessions, coaching sessions, and counselling.

Formal training

Formal training will prepare volunteers for specific jobs. Sometimes this can be quite lengthy, particularly when a volunteer lacks the specific skills required by the position. Crisis Lines, for example, provide many hours of training in how to deal with callers.

A volunteer who is recruited to drive elderly clients to medical appointments might be trained as follows.

Do

◆ be on time or notify the programme coordinator at least three hours in advance if you are going to be late;

◆ help patients in and out of the car, using the recommended method of assisting patients from a wheelchair into the vehicle;

◆ be familiar with the city;

◆ have a roadworthy and inspected vehicle.

Don't

◆ volunteer to assist clients with in-home chores;

◆ offer to take clients to other appointments on an unscheduled basis;

◆ take clients shopping;

◆ tell clients about the medical conditions of others;

◆ offer medical advice.

If

◆ there is a medical problem en route, go immediately to the nearest emergency room, the locations of which are marked on your map;

◆ the client asks for your opinion of her doctor, tell the client you aren't qualified to make such a judgment.

These hours may be spread over a couple of weeks. One programme for counselling delinquent children requires one evening of training per week for a year, before volunteers can begin working with clients. Volunteer firefighters in the US typically attend training once a week to polish up and expand their skills for as long as they are with the fire department.

Training can be presented in a variety of ways – through lectures, readings, discussion, field trips, videos, demonstrations, role-playing, case studies and so on.

There are two main areas to cover in volunteer training, regardless of the job for which the training is being provided.

The first is to communicate to the volunteer:

1. this is what you should do and accomplish in your job;
2. this is what you should not do;
3. this is what you should do in the following situations ... .

The content of the training provides the volunteer with the collected experience (both positive and negative) of previous volunteers. The content should be developed with the assistance of staff and volunteers who are familiar with the work, and the session might be delivered by these same staff or volunteers.

The second area might be termed a description of roles and responsibilities. It would include training which communicates to the volunteer the web of relationships in which they will be working:

1. this is with whom you will be working and this is your task;
2. this is their role and how it fits into the task.

For example, this could include telling volunteers who their supervisor will be and any other staff or volunteers who will be assigned to work with them. For example, a volunteer working in concert with others to serve a particular client, should be introduced to those volunteers and learn what each is providing to that client and how their efforts unite.

Benefits of training a volunteer

Training might also be developed for the volunteer programme because it serves as a tangible benefit that can be offered to the volunteer. Such training could be:

♦ training in ancillary skills
♦ training in career/life development
♦ cause-related training.

The training might be developed by the organisation by providing an opportunity for the volunteer to attend outside conferences or workshops. Attendance would be both an opportunity to increase knowledge, and a formal recognition by the organisation that the volunteer is worth the expense of sending them on such courses.

Young volunteers, who might have come to volunteering as a means of gaining career experience, might be offered sessions on computer skills, CV writing or career planning.

You should remember that training of any kind is almost always viewed with approval by volunteers. One of the primary benefits you can provide a volunteer is additional information, skills, or assistance in performing their work more productively, but you might also provide training in other areas of their life. Do not hesitate to ask for an additional commitment or effort from the volunteer in return for such training, since most of them will regard it as well worth the effort. To the volunteer, your interest in them is regarded as a recognition of the significance and importance of their contribution to the work of the organisation.

COACHING

Coaching is a process of teaching or upgrading skills. It can be used in formal training sessions or in on-the-job training. It will most often be provided by the supervisor of the volunteer or a more experienced co-worker. Effective coaching follows a three-step process:

1. a demonstration of the skill to be learned or improved

2. observation of the volunteer trying out the skill

3. feedback and analysis.

The skill can be demonstrated by anyone expert in that area. Either the person demonstrating the skill or the supervisor, trainer, or volunteer programme manager, should explain why the expert is doing what she is doing. The point of the demonstration is not just to allow the volunteer to see what is being done but to understand it.

To take an extremely simple example, if you were to demonstrate to a volunteer how to answer the telephone, you might have the volunteer watch you answer the phone a few times; then you might observe the volunteer answering the phone; finally you might have the volunteer answer the phone without being observed. After each stage you would discuss the experience with the intention that the volunteer learn from it.

The EIAG process

To increase your chances of the volunteer learning, these discussions can follow a learning model called EIAG. This stands for Experience, Identify, Analyse, Generalise, which are the four major steps people go through to learn things. If you keep these steps in mind as you coach volunteers, you can make sure they get the most from the learning process.

Experience

People generally learn from experiences, be they training exercises or real events. However, sometimes people have the same experience over and over again and never learn anything from it. If a person is to learn from an experience, their minds go through three additional steps.

Identify

If a person is to learn from an experience, they have to be able to describe it. In the simple example above, of learning to answer the phone, some questions you might ask are:

◆ what did I do?

◆ what did you do?

◆ how did the other person react?

◆ how have things been going for you?

◆ what has been happening?

Analyse

If a person is to learn from the identified experience, they must be able to analyse it. You want to get the volunteer to explore the factors in the situation that produced the experience. To continue with the example, some questions you might ask to help the volunteer analyse the steps are:

◆ why did I begin by saying 'Good morning?'

◆ what advantages are there to giving your name?

◆ why did the caller get so upset?

◆ why have things been going so well?

Generalise

If a person is to learn anything useful from an experience, they must be able to come up with some general rule or principle that applies beyond the specific situation to other, similar situations. Again, an effective coach relies on questions in this step. Some examples are:

◆ what will you do when you encounter a situation like this?

◆ what would you do differently if you had to do it over again?

◆ what would you advise someone else who is about to do this?

◆ what will you do to make sure things continue going so well?

As you begin to use the EIAG model, it is important that the sequence of questions you use be natural. Sometimes you may have a tendency to get locked into a prepared sequence of

An example of EIAG

EXPERIENCE ◆ IDENTIFY ◆ ANALYSE ◆ GENERALISE

As stated previously, coaching is particularly important with a volunteer who is new to a skill or concept. Imagine, for example, that you are a teacher of handicapped children and that you have a volunteer named Michael. You want Michael to help a child named Johnny learn to put his coat on and take it off. Although Michael has some experience in working with handicapped children, he has never done anything like this before. So you start by having Michael watch you work with Johnny. Afterwards, you use the EIAG technique to discuss things with Michael. Some questions you might ask include:

◆ what did you see me do with Johnny? (*identifying*)
◆ why did these techniques work better than others I tried? (*analysing*)
◆ what techniques seemed to work well? (*identifying*)
◆ what problems did I encounter? (*identifying*)
◆ why do you think these occurred? (*analysing*)
◆ what do you think you could do to avoid such problems? (*generalising*)
◆ based on what you saw, what are the things you will avoid and the things you will do when you work with Johnny? (*generalising*)

Once you are confident that Michael has a grasp of what to do, you watch him carefully while he attempts to conduct the lesson. During this time, if it seems like Michael is doing something that will upset or harm Johnny in any way, you would of course interrupt and suggest a different course of action. Or you might take over the lesson again yourself. In any case, after Michael's attempts, you would again ask questions to help him learn and grow from his experience:

◆ how would you describe what happened? (*identifying*)
◆ why did you put your coat on? (*analysing*)
◆ what were the strengths of your approach? (*analysing*)
◆ why did Johnny slap the coat out of your hand? (*analysing*)
◆ based on this insight, what will you do differently next time? (*generalising*)

In the course of this, you may need to go back and demonstrate the skill yourself, with Michael watching. You would then go back to watching him. Eventually, when you are comfortable that Michael has mastered the skill, you would allow him to work without watching. Nonetheless, you would continue to check on his progress from time to time, using the EIAG questions to make sure he is continuing to grow in his abilities. The checking would include direct observation, and reports from Michael. Eventually, you would be comfortable enough to rely simply on Michael's observations.

questions while a volunteer's response might naturally bring up others. If you have prepared a series of identification questions, don't ask them all in a row if you get an unexpected response on the first one. It might be better to go on and analyse that response than to proceed with your other questions.

The EIAG coaching model is effective because it is a natural one. It merely makes conscious the subconscious method you employ all the time. When you employ it, you are merely making sure that your volunteers complete all the steps in the learning process instead of leaving it up to chance. It also enables you to spot erroneous conclusions volunteers might reach from their limited experience. If, in the example opposite, Michael generalises that 'Johnny is simply incapable of learning anything', you might respond by getting him to analyse that statement: 'Why do you say that?'. You might give him sympathy for the difficulty of the task and encouragement to try harder. But above all you need to bring him to a different generalisation based on the facts, asking questions such as:

◆ is there anything else in the situation that might have caused that problem?
◆ what does seem to get Johnny's attention?
◆ can you think of any way to use that in the lesson?
◆ what will you try tomorrow?

COUNSELLING

In addition to orienting the volunteer and providing them with the skills to do the specific job, it is important to offer support or counselling throughout the volunteer's time with your organisation. The goal of counselling is to help the volunteer solve a problem or improve their approach by getting them to acknowledge a difficulty and take responsibility for the improvement.

The counselling process

When a volunteer encounters a problem in their work or during training, they may feel that the volunteer aspect of their life is no longer under control. When people feel a lack of control they get frustrated and their self-esteem suffers, which can lead to volunteer turnover. The goal of the counselling process is to restore a feeling of control in the volunteer's life by helping them find a course of action that will solve the problem.

As with coaching, the supervisor can use questions to help the volunteer do the following things.

Identify the problem
◆ What is going wrong?
◆ What exactly is happening?

Identify the cause of the problem
◆ What is causing the problem?
◆ Can you identify specific factors in the situation that are producing the problem?

Identify alternatives
◆ What else could you do?
◆ Have you considered this course of action? (making a suggestion)
◆ What would happen if you tried that?
◆ Then what would happen?

Identify a better course of action
◆ What are the strengths and weaknesses of each alternative?
◆ What can you do to solve the problem?
◆ Why do you think that might work?

Learn from their experiences
◆ What can you do differently in the future to avoid this problem?

Whilst it is fine to offer additional information or suggestions for courses of action that the volunteer might not see, however, you should not be telling the volunteer what to do. Your role is to make suggestions from which the volunteer then generates their own solutions. In this way the volunteer has a sense of ownership over the solution. The conversation might go something like this:

◆ *'Have you considered this course of action?'*
  'Oh, so that's what you want me to do?'

◆ *'Not necessarily. Have you considered that?'*
  'No.'

◆ *'What would happen if you did that?'*
  'I'm not sure.'

◆ *'Do you see any risks of that approach.'*
  'No. I guess it might work.'

◆ *'Why do you think it would work?'*
  'The clients wouldn't have to wait so long. And we would have more time to process their paperwork.'

◆ *'So what do you think?'*
  'I think it sounds like a good idea.'

◆ *'Let's see how it goes.'*

SUMMARY

Regardless of whether you are using formal training, coaching, counselling, or a mixture of methods, remember that the point is to make sure that volunteers feel happy and comfortable working for you organisation and that they learn and benefit from their experience. Satisfied volunteers are more likely to remain with your organisation and encourage others to volunteer.

CHAPTER EIGHT
Supervision

Once you have recruited your volunteers you will need to monitor their progress. This chapter outlines the techniques needed to manage your supervision of volunteers effectively. It also tells you what to do if things go wrong.

MANAGING PEOPLE

The effective volunteer manager should be good at managing people for two reasons. Firstly, they may be supervising volunteers who help manage the volunteer programme. In addition, they must make sure that staff do a good job of managing the volunteers they are working with. Both of these areas demand knowledge of managing the relationship between volunteers and those they are working with and responsible to. The most important element in this is the degree to which volunteers are empowered to make decisions regarding their work.

Topics covered include:

◆ **Creating a motivating environment for your volunteers**

◆ **Managing people by asking questions, rather than by telling them what to do**

◆ **Evaluation and feedback of a volunteer's performance**

◆ **Managing special categories of volunteers – including volunteers at a distance, professionally skilled volunteers and those volunteering as a group**

◆ **Firing a volunteer – and the alternative**

The manager's job is not to do things directly but to make sure things get done. Or, to put it another way, the manager's job is to do things that enable others to do the work.

In order to succeed in this, managers must learn to work through other people, however, most people who become volunteer managers are more used to doing things themselves. Unfortunately, the instincts that serve you well in getting work done yourself, are often counterproductive when it comes to getting things done through others.

Creating a motivating environment

Volunteer managers succeed primarily by creating conditions that encourage volunteers to want to do the work. By building a job around the volunteer's needs, as described previously, you begin by placing the volunteer in a job they want to do. Further, you tap into the volunteer's need for achievement by making sure there are goals, thereby providing the volunteer with a challenging responsibility that is likely to be satisfying. This can be done using several techniques that empower the volunteer.

By empowering volunteers, we mean making them more autonomous, more capable of independent action. The wisdom of this approach is that it is easier to get good results from empowered people than from people who are dependent. You can do this by giving them authority to decide, within limits, how they will go about achieving the results for which they are responsible. In such a relationship, the manager becomes a source of help for the volunteer rather than a controller. This not only feels better for the volunteer but allows the manager to spend less time making decisions about the volunteer's work and more time to think about overall strategy.

Levels of control

In giving people authority over the 'how' of their jobs, the danger is that they will do the wrong things. This danger is reduced by recognising the different degrees of authority volunteers can exercise in carrying out their responsibilities. The four levels of control described below define how much say the supervisor and the volunteer each have in deciding how each result is to be achieved.

1. Self-assignment

Self-assignment means that the volunteer decides what to do, does it, and that is the end of it. A person working as a tutor in a literacy programme, for example, might meet with a client at the client's home, conduct tutoring, and go home. Next week, they repeat this routine. They would do this without bothering to inform the paid staff what they had done or the progress they had made with the client.

This type of complete volunteer control rightly sends shivers of anxiety up the spine of most managers. The supervisor has no guarantee that the volunteer did the right things or indeed did anything at all. A lesser degree of volunteer control might therefore be more appropriate.

2. Monitoring progress

The volunteer decides what to do and does it, but at some point (the frequency of which is determined by the supervisor) they tell their supervisor what they did (either orally or in writing). If the volunteer did the wrong thing or the right thing in the wrong way, their supervisor finds out about it and can take steps to sort matters out. This gives the supervisor a bit more assurance that things will be done properly.

The frequency of progress reports depends on how anxious the supervisor is about the volunteer's performance. In the above example, if the supervisor has great confidence in the volunteer, they might only check progress once a month, finding out how the tutoring had gone, what the client had learned, what problems were encountered, how they were handled and what materials were needed. Moderate anxiety might require a report after each session. If a supervisor has high anxiety and the volunteer works at the organisation, she might check mid-way through the shift as to what has been accomplished thus far. A higher degree of anxiety might warrant a greater degree of control.

These progress reports need not be written. A simple, informal, chat between the supervisor and the volunteer is sufficient for the supervisor to be assured that things are going well.

3. Prior approval

If the supervisor is very anxious about the volunteer's performance and is worried that they are going to have to take steps to resolve this more often than is desirable, then they might want the volunteer to discuss with them beforehand what they intend to do.

When a volunteer is operating at this level of control, they are still the source of their own assignments. However, before they take action, their ideas are approved by the supervisor. The supervisor has pretty much complete assurance that the volunteer will do the right thing, because they have a veto over the volunteer.

There are various ways of approaching this. In some cases, a volunteer might provide daily recommendations – 'I suggest I call these people now', for example. On the other hand, the recommendation may be longer term, such as 'here is my plan to raise the client's reading level'. These gradations depend again on the supervisor's degree of anxiety about the volunteer's performance in pursuing particular targets.

At this level of control, the volunteer's regular progress report should also contain a plan for future action.

4. Control

If the supervisor's degree of anxiety about a volunteer's performance is extremely high, they might be tempted to allow still less control, or even no control at all.

At this level of control, the volunteer simply does what they are told. The authority for deciding what the volunteer will do is transferred from the person actually doing the work to management. This inevitably produces more work for the manager. The more people the manager supervises, the more time they will have to spend deciding what people should be doing.

Besides taking more time, this style of management reduces the number of creative ideas you get from volunteers. Good ideas for improving services will seldom surface if the volunteer is not expected to think. Volunteers, partly because they are not submerged in the day-to-day details of running the organisation, can provide a valuable perspective on the changing environment and the innovations needed to keep up-to-date.

Ideally, the only time you should use this level of supervision is when volunteers are new to the work. When people first come on board, they usually don't know enough about the organisation or the work they will be doing to make an intelligent recommendation. Usually, the volunteer knows this and wants to be told what to do. For this reason, it is appropriate to manage short-term volunteers in this way. If the volunteer stays for a while, however, you run a great risk to volunteer morale if you continue to deny them the authority to think for themselves.

Climbing the control ladder

The four levels of control are a ladder for people to climb. When a volunteer learns enough about the job to give an intelligent recommendation, they can be moved to level three.

As the volunteer progresses up the control scale, the amount of time you have to spend managing them decreases. Level four people take the most time because you have to do all the thinking, tell them what to do, and then check their progress. Level three people take less time because they do the thinking, they tell you what they intend to do, and then you check the progress. At level two, you simply check the progress.

Of course the ultimate in time saving is level one, where you don't even have to check the progress. However, this level has many obvious dangers. One is that the volunteer may think you aren't interested in their work and may feel undervalued and drop out. Another is that they may come to feel less connected to the programme and lose the sense of belonging that is so important to so many people. And of course, there is always the possibility that even the most trusted and proven volunteer might create a disaster that at level one strikes without warning.

Many managers see only two of these four levels of control, and they see the wrong two. For many, the only alternative to telling people what to do is to turn them loose. At level four you will reap resentment, but at level one you risk chaos. Most volunteers should work at either level three or level two.

Checkpoints

One of the most common management mistakes is the failure to check progress. Unless the volunteer is at level one, the supervisor should always keep track of what the volunteer has been doing. Even where the two parties have discussed in advance what was to be done, it is better to ensure the volunteer is making progress toward the target, than to wait until the end to be surprised that the result was different from what you expected.

A calendar, on which meetings or telephone conversations are scheduled is usually the easiest, cheapest, and most effective of all management controls. By requiring regular progress reports, you gain three important advantages, not least of which is that it lets people know you are serious about their achievements.

Progress reports also help avoid crises and poor quality, last minute work. This is particularly important on long-term projects where volunteers are expected to be self-starters. Most people start each day asking themselves 'What is the most urgent task I have to do today?'. If the volunteer project is not due for six months, it is easy to put off progress today, and this will continue to happen until the due date is excruciatingly near. But if the volunteer knows they have to report progress tomorrow, they will regard the project with a greater sense of urgency today. By setting regular checkpoints, you ensure that volunteers make regular progress.

A further advantage of regular reports is that they enable the manager to spot problems while there is still a chance for corrective action. If the volunteer has misunderstood your intentions, for example, you can find this out early, before they waste a lot of effort going in the wrong direction.

A common pitfall in reporting progress is when volunteers provide their own assessment of what they did rather than telling you what they actually did. If the volunteer says 'things went really well' this does not give the supervisor any information about what actually happened. When volunteers say 'things are fine', they are saying things are going the way they pictured them. The wise supervisor finds out if things are going the way THEY pictured them going.

MANAGING BY ASKING QUESTIONS

To get the best results, a good manager will ask a lot of questions. This helps the volunteer to feel involved, whilst leaving the questioner still very much in control.

Insecure, inexperienced supervisors think they should have all the answers. Whenever they interact with a volunteer, they feel that if they can't provide an answer to all the questions and have instant solutions for all the problems, they are failing. Such managers either make ill-considered decisions or make an excuse for a delay when presented with complex problems.

The root of this behaviour is the traditional manager's concern that the volunteers should have confidence in them. By contrast, an effective manager is most concerned that volunteers have confidence in themselves.

A volunteer who depends on her supervisor for all the answers does not grow on her own. Further, since such managers often think it is their job to tell volunteers what to do and how to do it, they tend to foster apathy and resentment. Volunteers in such circumstances tend to stagnate, grow bored or unsatisfied and move on.

The process of management can be divided into three main functions: planning, empowering, and evaluating. For each function there are several key questions to ask.

Planning questions

Planning refers to the manager's role in setting goals and making sure that the volunteer knows what to do. It is something managers should never do on their own; they should always involve the people who will be carrying out the plan, in order to give them a sense of ownership of the plan. You also make sure that the plan is based on the practical realities your volunteers face day-to-day. And you increase the likelihood that your people will pursue the plan with enthusiasm.

Some key planning questions include:
◆ what is the purpose of our work?
◆ what obstacles do we face in achieving that purpose?
◆ what resources do we have available to help us achieve our purpose?
◆ what strategies can we employ to overcome our major obstacles?

- what new developments affect us?
- how can we take advantage of new developments and trends?
- if we were to start the project all over again from scratch, what would we do differently?
- what problems are looming?
- what opportunities are presenting themselves?

In groups larger than six or seven, the manager will find it easier to increase active participation by having small groups of volunteers meet to discuss these questions and then report their conclusions to the whole group. With the data generated in response to these questions, the manager brings the group to focus by asking questions such as:

- based on all this, what should we be trying to accomplish?
- what should our goals be for the forthcoming period?

In all this the manager should not play a purely facilitative role. They may have strong opinions of their own. The manager should always get the most out of the group first. They should question first, suggest second, and only third state their own opinion. The idea is to encourage the volunteers to take ownership of the ideas, but to stay in control and ensure that effective goals are set.

At this point, however, no one has responsibility for any specific goal. A powerful next move is to refer to each goal and ask the question 'Who will take responsibility for achieving this goal?'. Again, the manager may have particular people in mind, and can certainly exercise her prerogative when assigning responsibility. But where appropriate, asking for voluntary assumption of responsibility leads to more committed pursuit of the organisation's objectives.

Other planning questions are appropriate after goals have been set and responsibility assigned or taken. At meetings with the responsible individual or team, the following questions can be asked:

- when can you submit your plan for achieving these goals?
- how will you measure your success?
- what is your timetable?

Questions can also be used to encourage volunteers to set short term goals for themselves and to maintain a sense of purpose on a daily basis. Questions in this regard include:

- what do you intend to accomplish this month?
- what can you do today to make progress toward your goals?
- what can you do today that will make the most difference?

Empowering questions

These questions can be used in counselling and coaching volunteers on job performance and motivational issues. They include:

◆ how do you feel about your job?
◆ what are your frustrations?
◆ do you know what you want to achieve? What do you need to do your job better?
◆ would you like more responsibility?
◆ is there something you would rather do than what you do here now?

When volunteers encounter difficulties or setbacks, they tend to get discouraged and drop out. They tend to focus on what they can't control, namely their past actions, and begin to feel frustrated and helpless. To avoid this, you need to prevent them focusing on what they did in the past and instead focus them on what they will do differently in the future. The main question you should ask about past difficulties is:

◆ what can you learn from this to help you in the future?

You might then want to probe a bit more, asking questions such as:

◆ why do you think this problem exists?
◆ what alternatives do you see?
◆ what are the strengths and weaknesses of those alternatives?
◆ is there a more productive way to look at this situation?

More importantly, however, you want to direct them quickly to future action, and to the things they can control. Questions to focus volunteers on future action include:

◆ what action do you recommend to solve the problem?
◆ what can you do to get back on target?
◆ what single step will start to make this situation better?
◆ what do you wish would happen?
◆ what could you do to make those wishes a reality?
◆ how could you get closer to the desired situation than you are today?

Evaluation questions

These questions attempt to evaluate the effectiveness of the volunteer's performance. Questions that help do this include:

◆ how would you evaluate your performance?
◆ are you on-target?
◆ if not, what went wrong?
◆ if so, how did you do it so well?
◆ what are the best ways of doing what you do?

These questions ask the volunteer to evaluate their own performance and the reasons for it. They encourage the volunteer to do a self-assessment and take their own corrective action.

Questions for yourself

Being a manager means being concerned about the ability of your people to fulfil their responsibilities to the organisation and its clients. Some questions to ask yourself from time to time to make sure you are paying attention to your responsibilities include:

◆ do my volunteers know what they're supposed to achieve?

◆ do they have sufficient authority to achieve it?

◆ do I and they know if they are succeeding or not?

◆ do they have the skills and knowledge necessary to succeed?

◆ are things organised so that their responsibilities are clear?

◆ how long has it been since I gave each of them any recognition for their contributions and achievements?

If you get negative answers to the first five of these questions, it means you have probably been spending too much time doing your own work and not enough time managing others. If your volunteers don't know what they are supposed to accomplish, for example, you have some goal-setting to do. If they lack skills, you have some training to do, and so on. If your answer to the last question is more than two weeks, you should make a special effort to let volunteers know that they are appreciated.

EFFECTIVE DELEGATION

One of the primary responsibilities of the manager is to delegate responsibility. In a volunteer management system, delegation can take a number of formats: volunteer manager to volunteers; organisation staff to volunteers; and volunteers to volunteers.

When delegating tasks to volunteers, the following elements ought to be included.

Define the assignment in terms of results

Delegation is the art of giving a person the authority to carry out a mutually agreed task. The most fundamental skill involved is defining the task. This should be phrased in terms of an outcome or something to accomplish. It should define the desired end-product, not the means of achieving it.

For example, imagine that one of the tasks on your list is to visit an electronics fair to see if there is any new equipment your organisation might profit from. Instead of telling the volunteer to go to the exhibition to see what new equipment is available, you could delegate the desired outcome of the activity. You might say something like 'I would like to give you the responsibility for upgrading our equipment', or 'I wonder if you would be willing to take the responsibility for improving our efficiency through the purchase of new equipment'.

Delegating by telling someone to go to the electronics fair removes one task from your list of things to do. Delegating by defining the result you want to achieve removes all the tasks related to that result.

Define the level of control

The second step in delegating effectively is to define how much authority the person has in carrying out the responsibility. This involves choosing from the four levels of control described earlier. Keep as much authority for deciding how to do the work in the hands of the worker as is possible.

To continue the example above, you might say 'I would like to see your plan for doing this before you get started', thereby placing the volunteer at level three. 'Let's get together every Friday for a chat about your progress on this', puts the volunteer at level two.

Communicate any guidelines

If there are relevant policies, laws, or regulations that the volunteer should work within, it is important to communicate these clearly at the outset.

To continue our example, the organisation may have purchasing regulations that need to be adhered to, such as getting price quotations from at least three suppliers. The volunteer needs to know this before wasting time doing something that would fall outside the rules.

Make resources available

If you know of any resources that would make the job easier or that would increase the chance of success, you should mention these at the outset. Resources can be people, manuals, events, institutions, and equipment, and should also include the budget, if any, for the task. At this point, you should stress that if the volunteer encounters difficulty, they must come to you for advice. When giving advice, however, it is important to make sure that you keep the authority for the work in the hands of the worker; that, if at all possible, you avoid telling the worker what to do.

In our example, you would want to tell the volunteer where the electronics fair is. You would also refer them to any staff with expertise in this area. Above all, you would tell them how much money was available for the project: 'Don't waste your time looking at anything that costs more than £1000', for example.

Determine criteria for success
The volunteer should know, at the outset, how the work will be judged. They should be involved in determining the criteria, and should have access to the data that indicates success or failure to fulfil the responsibility.

In our example, you might say that the organisation wants a piece of equipment that will pay for itself in a year's time.

Set up checkpoints
Unless the volunteer is at level one on the control scale, they should note on a calendar when they will be expected to report progress to you. The frequency of these checkpoints depends on your anxiety about the volunteer fulfilling the particular responsibility. These should not be presented to the volunteer as an excessively formal review meeting. Rather, it is an informal chat so you can find out how things are going.

MAINTAINING COMMUNICATION
It is desirable to provide on-going supervisory support for the volunteer. There are two main elements to any system of on-going support.

Availability
Supervisors must be available to volunteers. The volunteers must have the ability to meet with, report to, and talk with supervisors, both on a regularly scheduled basis (checkpoints) and at times of the volunteer's choosing.

If the supervisor is available to the volunteer, the volunteer will feel that their work is appreciated enough to merit the attention and time of the supervisor. Availability also encourages the volunteer to consult with the supervisor when and if they encounter difficulties.

Supervisors can schedule office hours during which volunteers can make appointments. Specific meetings for groups of volunteers can be scheduled for open discussions. Volunteers should also be able to approach their supervisor at any time. If you greet volunteers when they arrive for work and thank them when they leave this gives the volunteer a sense that you are approachable. The intent of all these methods is to develop a sense of open and ready communication and access.

Equal status and involvement

The second key element necessary to on-going supervisory support is a sense among the volunteers that they are being accorded equal status and involvement in the work of the organisation.

This equal treatment includes participation in decision-making (being invited to meetings or being asked for opinions, for example) and in day-to-day activities of the organisation (being on memo distribution lists, for example). To provide volunteers with a sense of being full partners in the organisation, they should be entitled to most of the benefits that staff are, such as access to training and trips, reimbursement of expenses, and proper job titles.

Perhaps the most challenging aspect is getting staff to remember volunteer's names. If people are addressed by name, they will feel like a somebody not a nobody. People often forget the name of a volunteer if they rarely work with them. One way to reduce this problem is to put pictures of volunteers and staff on a bulletin board or in a who's who directory so people can refresh their memories.

Volunteers will feel like second-class citizens if they are excluded from staff activities and benefits. These exclusions are often subtle, such as reserved parking for staff but not for volunteers, or no one ever thinking to invite volunteers to staff meetings. When volunteers feel they are less than staff, their self-esteem suffers, and they may stop wanting to volunteer.

Perhaps the most important aspect of building a sense of equality is open and free communication. This includes adding them to the newsletter mailing lists, making sure they are copied on correspondence that involves their work, or taking the time to update a volunteer on what has happened since they were last there.

Evaluation and feedback

Volunteer managers should develop a process for providing evaluation and feedback to volunteers. While often viewed negatively by those who have to administer it, a good evaluation process is actually of value to both volunteers and management, since it provides them with the feedback necessary to determine how well they are doing and suggestions on how to improve their performance. Regular evaluation sessions with volunteers are desirable both to help the volunteer work closer to their potential, and to help the organisation better utilise volunteers. Evaluation sessions should not deal with all the small performance problems that supervisors have been ignoring since the last evaluation session. This would distract from their main function, which is not day-to-day management.

Regular, scheduled feedback

Volunteers should receive feedback at regular intervals. The feedback should be more frequent when the volunteer first starts (monthly for the first six months) and then should be at least twice a year. The benefit of regular formal feedback is that it forces the supervisor to let the volunteer know how they are doing and how to improve. Too often, this feedback is put off by busy supervisors. In the absence of regular communication, performance issues tend to be avoided until minor difficulties turn into major problems.

A system established for providing this feedback would include the following steps:
- have a policy on performance appraisal and review;
- apply the policy to both volunteers and staff;
- develop performance criteria with each volunteer;
- explain expectations and procedures in advance.

One method for creating this system is simply to adapt the evaluation system in place for paid staff, assuming that there is an evaluation system for paid staff in operation.

Here are some tips for implementing the volunteer evaluation system:
- don't get overwhelmed by forms – the substance is more important than the paperwork;
- start with the job description – this should provide a basis for discussing what the volunteer has been doing;
- stick to the basics – job proficiency, working relationships, comparison with last review;

◆ listen at least as much as you talk – one way to look at the evaluation session is as a 'follow-up' volunteer interview, allowing you to see whether the needs and interests of the volunteer have changed enough to require a new assignment;

◆ remember that the evaluation may show as much what you need to do as what the volunteer needs to do.

The positive side of evaluation

Rather than thinking of evaluation as a system for dealing with problems, you ought to think of it as a means of rewarding those who are doing well. The percentage of volunteers who are troublesome is fairly small; the vast majority are hardworking. This means that the majority of evaluation comments can be positive ones, praising the work that is being accomplished.

The evaluation session can also be diagnostic in nature, allowing you to determine how volunteers are feeling about their work. For example, volunteers who are in demanding job positions (such as providing advocacy for abused children) often get burned out. Volunteers frequently fail to recognise such problems and or to ask for help, since their commitment drives them to continue to work. The evaluation session can provide the astute volunteer manager with the opportunity to determine whether a good volunteer is becoming exhausted, or bored, or needs to be transferred to another position. You can also find out a volunteer's readiness to be promoted to increased responsibility. The session thus becomes one of mutual evaluation, with the intent of rewarding and advancing those who have been productive.

SPECIAL CASES

There are several special situations which require particular care in supervision. Here are five examples which require some adaptation of the general principles listed above.

1 The assigned volunteer

An increasingly common situation involves the volunteer who is assigned to work directly with a particular member of staff, rather that being under the immediate control of the volunteer manager.

The staff member to whom the volunteer is assigned may neglect basic volunteer management functions, leaving the volunteer with a feeling of being stranded without any support. Some staff may engage in 'benign neglect', appreciating whatever work they obtain from the volunteer, but not viewing them as they would a paid employee doing an equivalent job, and to whom they would feel some supervisory responsibility. Some staff may engage in sporadic supervision, paying close attention to specific work assignments, but avoiding what they view as less important aspects of supervision, such as periodic evaluations.

The key to avoiding problems with assigned volunteers is for the volunteer manager to reach a clear understanding with those staff who are assigned volunteers, as to who performs what aspects of supervision and management. Areas of confusion include:

◆ who should complete a job description for the volunteer and who periodically reviews and updates it?

◆ who should interview potential candidates for the position?

◆ who should accept the volunteer for the position?

◆ who should complete the necessary paperwork and personnel forms?

◆ who will be responsible for on-the-job training of the volunteer?

◆ who will be responsible for providing work assignments for the volunteer, or for contacting the volunteer to inform them that no work is available?

◆ who will ensure that the volunteer is kept in touch with information and decisions relevant to their work?

◆ who will ensure that the volunteer has a work space and equipment?

◆ who will be available to talk to the volunteer if there is a problem?

◆ who will evaluate the volunteer?

◆ who should have the authority and responsibility to correct the volunteer's behaviour if there are problems, or to terminate the relationship?

◆ who will be responsible for the volunteer when the designated staff person is absent?

If volunteers are going to be working exclusively with a single member of staff, then it is essential to convey to that member of staff that they must act as the supervisor of the volunteer, and provide a link to the organisation and its work. This means that the member of staff must accept responsibility for providing the volunteer with work and working conditions that enable them to both be and feel successful.

2 The floating volunteer

Occasionally, volunteers are assigned to various parts of an organisation on a temporary basis, working with one group of staff today and tomorrow with another. While these volunteers will, over time, develop their own links with individual members of staff, it is recommended that the volunteer manager assume responsibility for most of the supervision of these floating volunteers.

Staff to whom the volunteer is temporarily assigned can provide supervision over direct job functions, but they will be unable to do more than this.

To avoid problems, the volunteer manager should take responsibility for the following:

◆ greeting the volunteer when they arrive at the organisation, and receiving the volunteer at the beginning of each new work assignment. They should also escort them to their new worksite and introduce them to the new staff with whom they will be working;

◆ acting as an on-going social and communication link between the volunteer and the organisation. This will mean making sure that the volunteer receives updates on organisation policy and decisions relevant to their volunteer job. It might also mean creating a small social group of other floating volunteers who meet periodically to keep in touch;

◆ providing on-going evaluation discussions, based on information gathered from staff with whom the volunteer has worked, and striving to find volunteer assignments that will meet the volunteer's changing talents and needs.

3 Long-distance volunteers

The long-distance or 'invisible' volunteer, who works in the field without day-to-day contact with the organisation and who may never even have been to the organisation's office, requires a different approach.

There are two challenges. The first is communicating with them, and the second involves making sure they are doing the right things. These issues of communication and control require a special effort on the part of the supervisor. Regularly scheduled weekly phone calls and regular updates from the organisation (newsletters, memos etc.), help to keep the long-distance volunteer informed and feeling part of the organisation. You can even ask the volunteer to contribute occasionally to your newsletter.

Communicating with long-distance volunteers

Here are some general tips for communicating with long-distance volunteers.

◆ Volunteers in isolated or distant settings will naturally have more communication problems than those who are gathered in one place. The smart supervisor will simply plan for this difficulty and adjust to compensate. Generally speaking, things will take longer, will have greater chance of being misunderstood, and will need to be managed more carefully.

◆ Volunteers in isolated or distant settings are prone to fears about exclusion from the system. They will worry about whether they are being kept properly informed of things (whilst decisions are being considered and after they have been made) and whether their input is sought and valued.

◆ Not providing information to your volunteers creates a sense of second class status. People from whom information is withheld will go to extraordinary lengths to either obtain the information or to create their own versions of what is going on.

◆ When decisions that affect particular people are being made, every effort should be made to involve those people in the decision-making process. Bringing people together for discussion is the best way to accomplish this. Technology can supplement but not totally replace face-to-face communication.

◆ Strive to achieve a sense of personal contact between headquarters and the field. People are more likely to communicate with those that they know and are more likely to forgive errors in communication. Bringing volunteers to visit headquarters is one way to accomplish this. Publishing a telephone directory with photographs is another.

◆ The longer it takes for a decision to be made at head office, the more left out people will feel. The more important the issue, the longer the response time will seem. Strive to get back as quickly as possible to those in the field, if only to deliver an interim response.

◆ Much communication takes place by osmosis - you learn things simply because you are in the vicinity of their occurrence. A supervisor at headquarters is in a much better position to learn via osmosis than a field volunteer. The smart supervisor proactively passes as much information as possible to the field. It is better to pass more information than is needed than to give the field a sense that you are restricting their access to information.

- Good communication should be viewed as a web connecting all within the system - it should function up, down, sideways and across. If you do not design your communication system to function this way, your volunteers will re-engineer it to do so, and will probably leave you out of their design.
- Uniformity should not be pursued as an end in itself. Use what works, which may be very different with volunteers in different situations.

Controlling long-distance volunteers

The second challenge can be met by setting clear goals for the volunteer, as described in the chapter on job design, and asking for frequent progress reports. To keep the volunteer feeling bonded to the organisation, consider having social events in which long-distance volunteers get together with staff.

The main tension between supervisors and long-distance volunteers is between the volunteer's need to decide what they will do and the supervisor's need to make sure that those things are done effectively. To minimise the conflict:

- establish clear priorities to guide volunteer's daily decisions. These priorities should give volunteers a clear sense of what is important and how their time should be spent – even when a supervisor is not around to give immediate instructions;
- ask volunteers to recommend observable, obtainable goals each month. These goals should relate to the established priorities;
- have regularly scheduled chats to check the volunteer's progress. Allocate your time and attention according to your experience with each volunteer. Direct more attention to those who have shown the need for monitoring or re-direction, but do not ignore the good performers simply because they are not causing problems.

It would also be well to remember when dealing with long distance volunteers that it is the same entrepreneurial traits (an ability to work alone, an ability to make decisions and be self-initiating) that make a long-distance volunteer successful which will make that same volunteer difficult to control. Supervisors may simply have to recognise that their ability to closely direct those who work alone in the field has different limitations than lies with those who work more contiguously.

4 Volunteer professionals

The fourth special case involves the supervision of professional volunteers, who are possessed of more expertise than the staff who are their supervisors. This imbalance in knowledge, experience, and sometimes even status, may make it difficult for staff to feel comfortable in exercising control over the professional, and for the professional to accept close supervision.

Step one in involving professionals as volunteers is job development. A common mistake is to assume that the professional should be the one who designs their own job, since they are the experts. While it is true that the professional can probably best determine how the work should be done, it is equally true that the other aspects of job design must be carried out with the involvement of the volunteer manager.

This includes determining what is to be accomplished, the desired results and why those results are important. Outlining these elements will both better motivate the professional and help them to decide how to best do the work. The more information you can provide about what you really need, the better they can match their knowledge and skills to your specific needs.

A further aspect involves setting the parameters of the job. This will include the desired timeframe for completion, available support systems, treatment of expenses, and needs for reporting and approvals. All of these will need to be discussed and negotiated with the professional volunteer, many of whom will be accustomed to exercising virtual autonomy over their work.

While this independence on their part works well for them, you may find it uncomfortable. A common problem is that their notion of expenses may not match your capacities. A lawyer may incur several hundred pounds worth of quite reasonable expenses in an afternoon, and be accustomed to billing these to clients. You, on the other hand, might find that amount to be larger than the entire budget for your project.

Another common problem lies in setting out what matters require approval. If, for example, plans need to be approved by the management committee before they can be implemented, then this should be made clear at the start, with an explanation of the system and timeframe for this process.

And, of course, if there are restrictions which will impact the shape of the job, these should also be outlined. If a computer programmer is designing a system to enhance organisation operations then any financial limitations need to be explained upfront.

Why employ professional volunteers?

Marlene Wilson, for example, relates a wonderful story of recruiting an advertising expert to help design a new brochure for an organisation. The expert was internationally acclaimed for their work, had agreed to help out, and eventually presented a suggested design. Marlene, who like most of us has her own preferences in style, started to make a few suggestions. The expert stopped her, and asked 'Why did you ask me to do this job, Marlene?'. After a moment she realised that it was because they were, in fact, the expert, which meant she might well keep her opinions to herself. The brochure, unchanged, went on to win several design awards.

In practice, more time needs to be spent on job design and negotiation with volunteer professionals than with most other categories of volunteers. Because the professionals are more likely to work independently and be self-supervising, it is imperative to have a clear mutual understanding of the desired results, parameters, and process of the volunteer work from the beginning.

Supervision of the professional volunteer may assume different forms. If you are working with large numbers of professionals, then it is sometimes helpful to recruit a lead volunteer from the group. They will act as your intermediary, and assume responsibility for supervision. This peer relationship will make it easier for them to deal with any problem situations.

For situations in which only one professional is recruited, then sometimes a quasi-buddy system works well. One person (sometimes a member of staff and sometimes a volunteer) is appointed to work with the professional, operating as primary liaison point with the organisation. This person monitors the progress of the work and helps the professional by retrieving information from the organisation, presenting reports, and so on. This informal supervision allows you to maintain some control of the situation without risking ego problems.

A common problem encountered in supervising expert professionals lies in the fact that you have recruited them for their expertise: they know how to solve the problem and you don't. This means that you must trust that expertise, which is often more difficult than it sounds.

The volunteer professional may have a much better idea of how well the job is progressing than you do, and any evaluation of the work may rely on their expertise. If the contribution of the professional is to be on-going or on an annual basis, then you might want to conduct an evaluation or de-briefing session, and review the work or project much like you would a special event, concentrating on how you can do things better in the future.

5 Groups of volunteers

A volunteer manager may occasionally involve a group of people, such as a club, as volunteers. This group will have its own identity, its own structure, and will view itself as volunteering as a group rather than as individuals. Keeping supervisory control over the actions of group volunteers can be a tricky job, as you have to keep a balance between the volunteers feeling ownership and responsibility, and having your organisation in control over what is done in its name. Consider the following as ways to juggle the two needs.

◆ When events or activities are to be done by group volunteers, offer clear, simple guidelines in a step-by-step fashion. Make sure the mission of the effort is clearly outlined. If there are any restrictions or requirements that need to be explained, let people know quickly. An example of this might be any restriction on the use of the organisation's name or logo, or any requirement for crediting corporate sponsorship. You don't want to wake up one morning and discover you're operating the IBM Food Bank Marathon because the group itself has gone out and got that support.

◆ If the project or activity has been done before, give the group all the information you have about what was done, what worked, and what didn't.

◆ Be clear about the various jobs that need to be done. For complex efforts, provide sample job descriptions and indicate how the tasks interconnect and work together toward the common goal.

◆ Clearly outline supervisory responsibility between you, the group, and its individual members. Make sure everyone is in agreement about who is in charge or what and of whom.

◆ Establish reporting dates and a channel for communication between you and the group. Meet more frequently early in the relationship so you can identify any problems or confusions.

◆ Get the group to appoint its own 'volunteer manager' with whom you will work. This is especially important for a one-off event. Work with this person to help them with recruitment, on-the-job supervision, and overall management. *Make sure that someone understands that they are in charge of overseeing the project.*

DISMISSING A VOLUNTEER

One of the recurrent nightmares of any volunteer manager is encountering a situation where they have to consider firing a volunteer. For many, this prospect creates severe stress, both over the appropriateness of the action and fear of possible legal and political consequences. Ann Cook, in a survey of Foster Grandparents Programmes in 23 communities in the US, found that 82% of responding volunteer managers rated the decision to terminate a volunteer as being a 'difficult or very difficult issue' for them. Over 60% of the volunteer managers reported delaying dealing with the problem.

This section is intended to provide some guidelines on developing a system that will assist you in confronting the problem and managing the decision to terminate a volunteer's relationship with the organisation.

Getting mentally ready

The first obstacle to overcome is to realise that dismissing volunteers is, in the appropriate circumstances, a necessary action. This is a difficult issue for many volunteer managers, usually because they are very people-oriented, and respect the willingness of others to help in their programmes. There is particular difficulty when the decision to terminate is not due to any particular fault on the part of the volunteer, but is instead due to ill health or a change in programme needs. Programmes where there has been a focus on volunteering as a benefit to the volunteer (such as some retirement volunteering programmes) also have great difficulty with this because they classify volunteers as 'clients', and it is philosophically difficult to justify terminating a client.

There are several rationales for dismissing volunteers. One is that the bottom line is the ability to deliver quality service to clients, and any barrier to that delivery is not allowable. This standard would apply to both paid and unpaid staff, as Jane Mallory Park points out: 'Whether the personnel in question are paid or volunteer, it is important to have policies and practices which promote accountability and the highest levels of performance possible without ignoring the reality that all individuals have idiosyncrasies and limitations as well as strengths. A double standard which does not give respect and dignity to both volunteers and paid staff is not only unnecessary but is also unhealthy for individuals and organisations'.

A second approach has to do with giving meaning and value to volunteer service. By denying that there is a right and a wrong way to do a volunteer job, one conveys the impression that the volunteer work is irrelevant and insignificant. An organisation which does not care enough about the work done by volunteers to enforce quality, communicates to other volunteers that their own work is meaningless.

The decision by an organisation to dismiss a volunteer is one that should be addressed before any need to do so arises. It should be discussed and ratified by staff and then codified as part of the overall policy statement on volunteer use and included as part of the organisation's volunteer policies.

ALTERNATIVES TO DISMISSAL

A decision to dismiss a volunteer should always be, in practice, a reluctant last resort. Firing a volunteer is an admission that volunteer management has failed. It means that the interviewing system did not work, or the job design was faulty, or that training and supervision did not operate the way it should. It is as much an indictment of the manager as it is of the volunteer.

It is crucial to remember that many situations that appear to warrant dismissal may actually be solved by less drastic measures. Before contemplating firing a volunteer, see if any of the following approaches may be more appropriate and less painful.

◆ Re-supervise

You may have a volunteer who doesn't understand that rules have to be followed. This is a common problem with youth volunteers, some of whom automatically test the rules as part of their self-expression. Enforcement may end the problem.

◆ Re-assign

Transfer the volunteer to a new position. You may, on the basis of a short interview, have mis-read their skills or inclinations. They may simply not be getting along with the staff or other volunteers with whom they are working. Try them in a new setting and see what happens.

◆ Re-train

Send them back for a second education. Some people take longer than others to learn new techniques. Some require a different training approach, such as one-on-one mentoring rather than classroom lectures. If the problem is lack of knowledge rather than lack of motivation, then work to provide the knowledge.

◆ Re-vitalise

If a long-time volunteer has started to perform poorly, they may just need a rest. This is particularly true with volunteers who have intense or demanding jobs, such as one-to-one work with troubled clients. The volunteer may not realise or admit that they're burned out. Give them a sabbatical and let them re-charge or transfer them temporarily to something that is less emotionally draining.

◆ Refer

Maybe they just need a whole new outlook of life, one they can only get by volunteering in an entirely different organisation. Refer them to the Volunteer Centre or set up an exchange programme with a sister organisation. Swap your volunteers for a few months and let them learn a few new tricks.

◆ Retire

Recognise that some volunteers may no longer be able to do the work they once could and may even be a danger to themselves and to others. Give them the honour they deserve and ensure that they don't end their volunteer careers in a way they will regret. Assist them in departing with dignity before the situation becomes a tragic crisis.

All of these alternatives are both easier to implement and managerially smarter than making a decision to fire a volunteer. They recognise that there are many reasons why a person may be behaving inappropriately and that some of these reasons have answers other than dismissal. We strongly urge that you consider each of these alternatives before deciding to fire any volunteer.

The three stages of dismissing a volunteer

If you do encounter a situation where none of the alternatives work, it is helpful to have in place a system for dealing with the problem. Some organisations have been sued by terminated volunteers (this possibility depends on whether the volunteer is deemed to have had a contract of employment under employment protection legislation) and dismissal may cause political and community relations problems. The system outlined below is designed to help the volunteer manager, both in making and justifying the decision to terminate a volunteer.

1 Forewarning/notice

The first stage of the system is to develop clear policies about the dismissal of volunteers. To do this you need to devise:

◆ a set of official personnel policies regarding the employment of volunteers, including policies on probation, suspension, and termination;

◆ a system for informing volunteers, in advance, about these policies. Volunteer induction should discuss the policies and provide examples of requirements and unacceptable behaviour;

◆ a mechanism for relating these policies to each volunteer job. This means having a job description for the volunteer which explains the requirements of the job, and has some measurable objectives for determining whether the work is being accomplished satisfactorily.

2 Investigation/determination

The second part of the system involves determining whether the volunteer has actually broken the rules. This implies having a fair investigator take the time to examine the situation and reach a decision that something has been done wrongly. You should never terminate a volunteer on the spot, regardless of the infraction. Instant firing doesn't allow you to recognise any extenuating circumstances. This is why a suspension policy is so important.

Essentially, the volunteer manager needs to establish a process for reviewing the performance of volunteers and recording problems. This should be done as part of the regular evaluation process. Those volunteers whose performance is unsatisfactory are told of their deficiency, counselled on improving their work, and then re-evaluated. Failure to conform to the quality standard over time can then become grounds for termination. In cases where the unsatisfactory performance is not incremental, but is substantial in nature (inappropriate relations with a client or breach of confidentiality) then what is needed is some proof that the volunteer did in fact commit the wrong-doing. This might be testimony from other volunteers, staff, or the client.

During this part of the process the volunteer manager also investigates whether any of the alternatives to firing would provide a more appropriate solution.

3 Application

This final part of the system requires that the volunteer manager do a fair job of enforcing the system. It requires equal and fair application of the rules (no playing favourites), appropriate penalties (graduated to the severity of the offence) and, if possible, a review process, so that the decision does not look like a personal one.

You will note that the above three processes mirror common personnel practices for paid staff. They are in fact the same, as they should be, since evaluating paid and unpaid staff should follow the same rules.

The advantages of this system are two-fold. First, it helps the volunteer manager to reach the right decision, and feel comfortable about making that decision. The system is fair to both the volunteer and the organisation if properly followed and tends to produce correct answers. It also allows the volunteer manager to use a less drastic solution where appropriate. Second, the system helps develop a case for dismissal that can be used to explain the decision to others, internally and externally.

Fortunately for volunteer managers, many problem volunteers decide voluntarily to resign rather than face the inevitable and seemingly inexorable conclusion of the dismissal process.

Conducting the dismissal meeting

Regardless of how the decision to terminate is reached, someone has to convey that decision to the volunteer. Fortunately, most supervisory experiences with volunteers will be pleasant, and you will spend more time assisting dedicated volunteers to maximise their performance. It is good, however, to be prepared for the exception, since it is one of the responsibilities of the effective volunteer manager to protect the programme and the other volunteers by dealing quickly and conclusively with problem volunteers.

◆ Conduct the meeting in a private setting. This will preserve the dignity of the volunteer and perhaps of yourself.

◆ Be quick, direct, and absolute. Don't beat around the bush. It is quite embarrassing to have the volunteer show up for work the next day because they didn't get the hint. Practise the exact words you will use in telling the volunteer, and make sure they are unequivocal. Do not back down from them even if you want to preserve your image as a nice person.

◆ Announce, don't argue. The purpose of the meeting is simply, and solely, to communicate to the volunteer that they are being separated from the organisation. This meeting is not to re-discuss and re-argue the decision, because, if you have followed the process above, all the arguments will already have been heard. You should also avoid arguing to make sure you don't put your foot in your mouth while venting your feelings. Expect the volunteer to vent, but keep yourself quiet.

◆ Don't attempt to counsel. If counselling were an option, you would not be having this meeting. Face reality; at this point you are not the friend of this former volunteer, and any attempt to appear so is misguided.

◆ Follow-up the meeting with a letter to the volunteer re-iterating the decision and informing them of any departure details. Make sure you also follow-up with others. Inform staff and clients of the decision, although you do not need to inform them of the reasons. In particular, make sure that clients with a long relationship with the volunteer are informed of the new volunteer assigned to them.

CHAPTER NINE
Retention and Recognition

Retaining your volunteers is the key to success. There is no point in being good at recruitment and training, if you cannot keep them. This chapter examines motivation and reward.

Topics covered include:

- **Understanding why people volunteer**
- **Giving your volunteers a sense of esteem**
- **Retention strategies for short-term volunteers**
- **Volunteer recognition**

MOTIVATION

As has been emphasised throughout this book, volunteer programmes are fuelled by the motivation of the volunteers and the staff of the organisation. Problems of volunteer retention can usually be traced to problems of motivation.

A motivated volunteer is one who wants to do the job that needs to be done in the spirit and within the guidelines of the organisation. People behave in motivated ways when the work satisfies a need of theirs. Motivation comes from inside the volunteer, stemming from a set of needs which are satisfied by doing things which they find productive and rewarding.

When you encounter a volunteer who is not behaving as you would like, you may label them unmotivated, but actually this is incorrect. A so-called unmotivated person will be just as keen as a motivated person: they also need, want, and desire something. However, for reasons we will explore in this chapter, those needs are met in counterproductive ways. They behave in a way which you may consider inappropriate, because doing so is more satisfying than the behaviour you would like them to choose. In other words, people behave the way they do for a particular reason.

> *"When we talk about motivating volunteers, we are talking about creating a volunteer experience which allows an individual to meet their motivational needs in ways that are productive for the organisation and satisfying for the individual. You remove barriers to motivation by designing satisfying work experiences and creating systems that allow volunteers to meet their needs".*

ask what they want to achieve, and set up a programme to help them achieve it.

Keep in mind that peoples' needs can change

All behaviour is motivated

Sometimes, unmotivated behaviour is caused by frustration. If a volunteer has a high need for achievement, for example, and they see little to accomplish in their job, they may choose to set up a win-lose situation with those in authority. For example, a volunteer might go to the board of trustees every time there is a disagreement, seeking to get the decision overturned. This so-called unmotivated behaviour met the volunteer's need for achievement. It provided a challenge. It gave an opportunity to win.

When we talk about motivating volunteers, we are talking about creating a volunteer experience which allows an individual to meet his or her motivational needs in ways that are productive for the organisation and satisfying for the individual. By designing satisfying work experiences, and creating systems that allow volunteers to meet their needs, you make sure that volunteers receive their motivational paycheck for the valuable contributions they make to your organisation. This is the essence of volunteer retention.

People are motivated in different ways

Because each volunteer has a different combination of needs, each will do best in different situations. One volunteer may be motivated by gaining work experience, whereas another may be motivated by the desire to meet new people, and a third may have a burning passion to contribute to the cause. For the first, you need to make sure that the volunteer has the opportunity to learn the skills they want to learn. The second must be placed in a work setting where they can work with others. The third will want a job in which they feel they are making a meaningful contribution to the organisation's mission.

This is further complicated by the fact that a volunteer's needs may change over time. For example, a volunteer may work well on an independent project. It satisfies her need to achieve something meaningful. Then her husband dies. Her need to be with others may suddenly become much more important than the need to achieve something meaningful. To satisfy this need and retain the volunteer, you might transfer her to a group project.

Each to their own mix

Volunteers have many needs. The art of motivating them lies not only in knowing how to tap a given motivation, but in being able to figure out what combination of needs a particular volunteer has. One way to do that is to ask the volunteers periodically. Discuss their rating of the relative importance of the following motivational factors:

◆ to gain knowledge of community problems

◆ to maintain skills no longer used otherwise

◆ to spend quality time with members of the family by volunteering together

◆ to get out of the house

◆ to make new friends

◆ to be with old friends who volunteer with the organisation

◆ to gain new skills

◆ to have fun

◆ to meet a challenge

◆ to improve the local community

◆ to work with a certain client group

◆ to be in charge of something

◆ to be part of a group or a team

◆ to gain work experience to help get a job

◆ to meet important people in the community

◆ to gain status with my employer

◆ to get community recognition.

The mix of responses from the volunteer will give you a better feeling for why they want to volunteer and what you need to give them in return as their 'motivational paycheck'. For example, if a volunteer ranks the last three above as their highest needs, you will need to make sure they have a job which does indeed enable them to meet important people and which is highly visible in the community. To make sure that her employer is aware of her contribution, you can send a letter of commendation for her contributions.

RETAINING VOLUNTEERS

The key to retaining volunteers is to make sure you are meeting their particular complex of motivational needs. When this is occurring across the volunteer programme, a positive, enthusiastic climate is created which, in turn, encourages people to continue to volunteer.

Giving volunteers a sense of importance

Retaining volunteers is largely a matter of making them feel valued and important. When the work environment boosts a person's self esteem, they feel good about the job, be it paid or volunteer work. They look forward to going to the workplace.

Psychologists Harris Clams and Reynold Bean have studied self-esteem for many years. They found that people with high self-esteem are those who simultaneously satisfy three particular motivational needs. They enjoy a sense of *connectedness,* a sense of *uniqueness,* and a sense of *power* or *effectiveness.*

Connectedness

When people feel connected, they feel a sense of belonging, of being part of a relationship with others. In a highly mobile society, where friends and loved ones may live hundreds of miles away and the nextdoor neighbour is sometimes a stranger, this need is often unmet, leaving people with a sense of isolation, dissatisfaction, and loneliness. The psychologist William Glasser points out that this need is often stronger even than the need to survive, in that most people who try to commit suicide do so out of loneliness.

The following factors are most often mentioned as producing a sense of belonging:

◆ a common goal
◆ common values
◆ mutual respect
◆ mutual trust
◆ a sense that one group member's weaknesses are made up for by another group member's strengths.

A sense of identification with a work group can meet this need, producing healthier, happier individuals. In our seminars over the past four years, we have surveyed more than 1500 individuals who at one time in their lives felt a positive sense of connectedness.

People with a sense of connectedness have a sense of 'we' as well as a sense of 'I'. The more special the 'we' is, the more special the individual feels as part of the group and the greater their self-esteem. This is why it is important to have high standards for becoming a group member.

Leaders of volunteer programmes should be on the look out for comments people make about the expectations they have of themselves and their co-workers. If people say things like 'I'm just a volunteer', or 'What do they expect for free?', it should cause alarm bells to ring. People's self-esteem drops when they regard themselves as part of a below average group. This lack of connectedness leads to high turnover of staff and volunteers. When they hear negative statements such as this, leaders should try to generate positive ideas for improving the situation. They might ask: 'What makes you say that? What can you do to improve this situation? What kind of place would you want to work in? What can you do to make this organisation more like the kind of place you want it to be?'.

Leaders should spread the word about positive accomplishments. They should talk about the values and standards of the organisation and what it means to be part of the group. They should look for opportunities to promote interaction among

---

Positive feelings of connectedness can be enhanced in volunteer programmes by many leadership actions, some of which have been referred to previously.

1　The volunteer manager can work with staff to make sure that there is a common purpose or goal for the team. Nothing is as fundamental to a team being effective, as a common sense of what they are trying to achieve together. Both staff and volunteers should see themselves as equal partners in pursuing this goal.

2　In developing jobs for volunteers (other than for one-off volunteers who you don't expect to retain) staff should avoid setting performance standards that are too low. If the expectations are too easy to meet, people will not feel special about their participation. Volunteers should not have lower standards than paid staff.

3　The volunteer manager should ensure that staff and volunteers are treated equally. The volunteer manager should be on the lookout for behaviour which inadvertently makes volunteers feel excluded. A common example is that volunteers are not invited to staff meetings, not because they are deliberately excluded, but because no one thought to invite them. Such a situation can make volunteers feel like second-class citizens.

4　When working with staff to develop jobs for volunteers, the volunteer manager should make sure that volunteers (or teams of volunteers) have a sense of ownership of a client or project. Fragmentation of ownership generates blame and criticism – which is the enemy of connectedness.

5　The volunteer manager should encourage leaders to celebrate the accomplishments of volunteers in context of their contribution to the goals of the group. Recognition must be consistent so that people do not suspect favouritism. Team accomplishments can also be celebrated, giving equal credit to all team members.

"In a truly positive climate, people feel safe to be who they are. They can behave in an individual manner and yet feel supported by the group. People respect each other for their unique strengths and eccentricities. They support each other unconditionally".

group members. This is particularly important where there are few natural opportunities for people to share their common experiences. For example, in befriending schemes and literacy programmes, volunteers will be working with the client and to their own schedule. Such volunteers work with little daily supervision and rarely appear in the office. Effective volunteer supervisors, knowing that 'it's lonely out there', take pains to bring these people together for training, pot lucks, and swapping of anecdotes.

Another way to promote interaction is to involve people in the decision-making process. When each group member feels they have a say in deciding the unit's strategy, their feeling of connectedness is enhanced. In such meetings, it is important that you do not let your own opinions be known in advance. Group members who know what the person in authority wants will tend to support that position. If you already know the way you want to go, you might as well just tell them.

People's sense of connectedness is enhanced by engaging in new experiences together. By insisting on constant improvement, leaders encourage people to try out new ways of doing things. If these are done by teams, the sense of connectedness grows.

Uniqueness

A second characteristic of people with high self-esteem is a feeling of uniqueness. This means that they feel special in some way; that they have a unique combination of talents and personal qualities.

Volunteer managers can build feelings of uniqueness by recognising the achievements of individual group members and praising them for their individual qualities. Encourage individuals to express themselves and, by giving them the authority to think, to explore alternative ways to achieve their results.

People's uniqueness can also be enhanced by giving them challenging assignments which take advantage of their individual strengths. 'This is a difficult responsibility requiring your special talents', a volunteer's supervisor might say. Such a statement, of course, should be their sincere belief.

This need to feel unique is sometimes in conflict with a person's need to feel connected. All of us tend to make compromises in our uniqueness in order to feel connected and sacrifice some connectedness in order to feel more unique.

Creating a positive climate is often difficult. It cannot be done without interaction between group members, or without shared values and a common purpose. It may require the services of an expert facilitator to lead a session in which people explore their differences and gain an understanding of everyone's unique point of view. It is always enhanced by leaders emphasising the strengths of individual members and their contributions to the group.

It is also enhanced by encouraging the individual development of each volunteer. Provide people with maximum training. As they learn new skills, their sense of individual competence grows. A common way to do this is to send them to conferences and workshops to keep them up to date with the latest developments in their field.

> **Unique or connected?**
>
> Imagine, for example, a volunteer named Julie. Part of her feeling of uniqueness revolves around her image of herself as a free spirit. This manifests itself in a variety of ways, such as wearing unusual clothing and jewellery. Her organisation's values, however, are quite traditional, and it is an accepted group norm to dress conservatively. Julie is faced with a choice between dressing conservatively to gain a sense of connectedness, thus sacrificing some of her uniqueness, or to continue her unique style at the risk of becoming something of an outsider to the group. Neither of these courses of action is fully satisfactory to her.

One idea is to have volunteers research a topic and present their findings to the others. This enhances the presenter's feelings of uniqueness – their special knowledge is being imparted to others – while also creating a sense of connectedness.

Effectiveness

Another aspect of positive self-esteem is a feeling that you are making a difference. This feeling is often stifled in traditional volunteer jobs. If people work in fragmented systems, doing menial tasks not connected to a final outcome, it is difficult for them to feel that they are making much of a difference. The self-esteem of people in such circumstances is reduced.

To feel effective, volunteers need to work on things that matter. If they are engaged in support activities, for example stuffing envelopes, they should be told the purpose of the mailing and the results that are achieved from it so they can feel they are doing something worthwhile.

Part of feeling effective is feeling in control. Managers often take this feeling away from people by trying to overly control their behaviour. Rather than defining results and allowing people some say in figuring out how to achieve them, managers tell people

> "To feel effective, volunteers need to work on things that matter. If they are engaged in support activities, for example stuffing envelopes, they should be told the purpose of the mailing and the results that are achieved from it so they can feel they are having an effect on something worthwhile".

exactly what to do. When one person attempts to control the behaviour of another, the result is rarely positive.

As explained in previous chapters, you can produce feelings of effectiveness by making volunteers responsible for results. They then have a sense of being in charge of something meaningful and having the authority to think for themselves.

The need to feel in control is often in conflict with a person's need for connectedness. People in teams sometimes yearn for more individuality. Their desire to influence others, and to have their own way, sometimes alienates other group members.

As Glasser points out in his book *Control Theory*, almost everyone goes through life trying to balance conflicting needs, making compromises that are never fully satisfactory. If you can create a situation in which these conflicting motivational needs are met simultaneously, you will unleash a tremendous sense of well-being in your volunteers and enthusiasm for the job.

Applying retention strategies to short-term volunteers

For many reasons, short-term volunteering is not as rewarding as long-term – it doesn't really provide the emotional satisfaction of being an integral part of something. Many short-termers may be engaging in a variety of volunteering, sampling what is available until they find the volunteer position which is right for them.

To take advantage of this, a smart volunteer coordinator should develop a series of entry-level, short-term jobs which provide the volunteer with the opportunity to see how they like working with the organisation, its staff, and its clientele. Once the volunteer is working in these starter jobs, the volunteer coordinator should work at keeping them, slowly grooming the volunteer for more work and ensuring that the volunteer truly enjoys the work they are doing. Volunteers are curiously rational: they won't stay in jobs that aren't enjoyable, but they will stay in those that are.

In the 1988 Gallup Poll on Giving and Volunteering in the United States, 14% of those volunteers who reported increasing their volunteer hours said they did so because of expanding interest and involvement in the work they were doing.

Evidence of the effects of this phenomenon is available from studies of volunteer behaviour. From this perspective, emphasis on volunteer retention is much more important than emphasis on recruitment. Rather than focusing on constantly bringing new volunteers into the system – with the added expenditure of energy required for recruitment, screening, orientation and training – this approach would concentrate on maintaining and retaining the existing volunteer force. Over time, the organisation will benefit from the increased experience levels of its volunteers and from the lessened costs of recruiting newcomers.

There are three different ways of improving volunteer jobs to make them more interesting and involving.

1 Give them a great place to work

The process for strengthening involvement necessarily varies from job to job, and from volunteer to volunteer, but some factors are common to all situations. One of these is providing a rewarding job for the volunteer, one in which working facilities are satisfactory and social relationships are positive.

Research has identified certain factors which might be important in this conversion process. A study of volunteer workers in three Israeli social service organisations found that organisational variables (such as adequate preparation for the task they were asked to do) and attitudinal variables (such as task achievement, relationships with other volunteers, and the nature of the work itself) were the best predictors of volunteer retention.

After analysing their data, the researchers noted:

'Perhaps the single most important finding reported in this study is the relatively high importance volunteers accord situational facilities.... In addition to the intrinsic and extrinsic incentives associated with volunteer work, then, it appears that individuals strongly desire conditions and organisational settings that facilitate effective and efficient volunteer work.'

Roughly translated, this means that volunteers like good working conditions, just like the rest of us, and that volunteers tend to prefer jobs where the environment is friendly, supportive, and effective.

The factors which are key elements for each volunteer job will vary. A study of the Master Gardener volunteer programme identified the three benefits which volunteers thought most essential: receiving new sources of information, obtaining new knowledge, and gaining access to experts and information. Note that none of these is altruistic. Each factor involves a benefit which the volunteer felt to be of value to themselves and which was gained through volunteering and the additional training provided.

2 Give them what they don't have

The best approach to making a job more interesting is to look at it from the perspective of the volunteer. What is it that they want out of their volunteering that they aren't getting from their paid job or elsewhere?

A study of volunteers at three social service organisations tested the hypothesis that some people volunteer in order to satisfy needs that are not being met by their paid employment. The findings indicated that volunteers whose regular paid employment failed to satisfy their needs for psychological growth tended to be more satisfied with volunteering when it could satisfy those needs.

One of the conclusions was particularly intriguing: "The present study suggests that volunteers who perceive their paying jobs as relatively unfulfilling should be asked to do the more challenging work".

This would suggest that volunteer motivation could be improved by first analysing potential volunteer's attitudes toward their current job and identifying deficiencies, then structuring volunteer assignments to fill the gaps. Variables that might be examined include whether the paid job is worthwhile, interesting, satisfying, diverse, flexible, provides social interaction, allows expression of leadership skills, and so on. Sample questions which could be used during the volunteer interview would include:

during interview

- ◆ what do you get out of your current job?
- ◆ what do you not get to do sufficiently in your current job?
- ◆ what would your ideal job look like?
- ◆ what would you do in it, and what would you not do?'

The prospective volunteer would be encouraged to identify elements that would meet motivational needs not currently met in their life and particularly not in their paid work. It would then become important to make sure that the volunteer job provided these needs.

3 Give them a good time

One of the easiest ways to retain volunteers is to make sure they have fun!

Henderson has suggested that volunteering can be viewed as a leisure activity – something which is done out of choice, and without expectation of monetary benefit. People have similar expectations of leisure and volunteering: 'People want to do something interesting, to achieve something, meet people, have fun, learn new things, be refreshed, and relax'. All of these factors might be examined as aspects of volunteer jobs which could be strengthened.

Henderson also suggests that the volunteer manager focus on four areas to take advantage of this relationship between leisure and volunteering:

- the self-interest and recreational expectations of volunteers which might make volunteering more appealing;
- providing volunteer opportunities which will be perceived as worthy leisure;
- utilising the 'recreative aspects' of volunteering as a technique for recruitment;
- matching a person's leisure expectations to potential outcomes associated with a volunteer experience.

[handwritten margin note: relate volunteering to leisure activities → take advantage.]

Focusing retention efforts

One way to encourage volunteer retention is to focus on critical points in the volunteer's relationship with the organisation. There are two critical periods, described below.

The first six months

Studies of volunteer retention have determined that the first six months experience of a volunteer is critical towards their retention. The greatest loss of volunteers occurs during this period, as volunteers resign or simply drift away and disappear.

[handwritten margin note: greatest loss]

The loss probably occurs because new volunteers have approached the organisation with certain expectations for what they will encounter and what they will be able to accomplish. If, in this initial period, there is a significant gap between their expectations and the actual situation encountered, the volunteer is more likely to decide to leave.

[handwritten margin note: initial → expectations not met]

Volunteer managers need to pay close attention to volunteers during this early period and help the transition through the normal ups and downs of this acclimatisation stage. They should also ensure that the volunteer does not have problems created by an inappropriate job match.

Anniversaries

Volunteers also require more attention at anniversaries, such as annual evaluation dates, the end of large projects, or the completion of an agreed term of participation.

At these critical points, the volunteer is likely to engage in a re-evaluation of their service to the organisation, reconsidering their commitment to, and interest in, the work that they are doing. You can help the volunteer re-affirm that commitment by pro-actively assisting them to identify new interests and goals, and then suggesting possible jobs within the organisation that will help the volunteer obtain these new motivational objectives.

Do not assume that a volunteer who has been doing a job will always want to do that same job. Volunteers change over time, due to changes in their own lives and exposure to certain types of volunteer work. Periodically review what they are doing to make sure they are still happy doing it.

Don't forget the obvious

Two final comments about retention: the first is so obvious that many programmes not only ignore it, they do exactly the opposite. Since volunteers are coming to the organisation because they want to help, it is essential that you do every thing you can to give volunteers work to do as soon as possible. Underutilisation creates serious retention problems, because motivated volunteers who are trying to be of assistance will feel useless if they are not actually involved in doing something. They will also lose any sense of relationship with the organisation over long periods of non-involvement.

The second is equally obvious: when in doubt, ask the volunteer what they want to be doing. Part of the original volunteer interview and part of every subsequent evaluation session should consist of ascertaining what the organisation might do that would meet the volunteer's motivational needs. This includes finding the right job for the volunteer, but it also includes identifying what it would take for the volunteer to feel successful in the job. Questions such as: 'how can we show you we care?'; 'what would it take to make you feel successful in this job?', and 'who would you like to know about your accomplishments?', are designed to uncover possible retention and recognition strategies. It is crucial to keep exploring this area because the motivational needs of the volunteer will undoubtedly change over their lifetime, and during the course of their relationship with the organisation.

RECOGNISING VOLUNTEERS

Volunteers must receive a sense of appreciation and reward for their contribution. This sense can be conveyed through a number of processes, including both formal and informal recognition systems.

Formal recognition systems

Formal recognition systems are comprised of the awards, certificates, plaques, pins, and recognition dinners or receptions to honour volunteer achievement. Many organisations hold an annual ceremony in which individual volunteers are singled out for their achievement.

In determining whether or not to establish such a formal ceremony, consider the following:

◆ Is this being done to honour the volunteer, or so that staff can feel involved and can feel that they have shown their appreciation for volunteers?

◆ Is it real, and not stale or mechanical?

◆ Does it fit? Would the volunteers feel better if you spent the money on the needs of the clients rather than on an obligatory luncheon with dubious food?

◆ Can you make it a sense of celebration and a builder of team identity?

Formal recognition systems are helpful mainly in satisfying the volunteer who has a need for community approval, but have little impact (and occasionally have a negative impact) on volunteers whose primary focus is helping the clientele. These volunteers may very well feel more motivated and honoured by a system which recognises the achievements of their clients, and also recognises the contribution which the volunteer has made towards this achievement.

Informal recognition practices

The most effective volunteer recognition occurs in the day-to-day interchange between the volunteer and the organisation through the staff giving their sincere appreciation and thanks for the work being done by the volunteer.

This type of recognition is more powerful in part because it is much more frequent – a once-a-year dinner does not carry the same impact as 365 days of good working relationships.

The intention of day-to-day recognition is to convey a constant sense of appreciation and belonging to the volunteer. This sense can be better conveyed by the thousands of small interactions that compose daily life than it can be conveyed in an annual event.

Recognition can begin quite early. A card of welcome sent to a new volunteer, or a small welcome party conveys an immediate sense of appreciation.

Matching recognition to types of volunteers

It is also possible to think about systems of volunteer recognition that are appropriate to particular types of volunteers.

1 Motivational orientation

One could think about recognition which was more appropriate for different basic motivational needs, as follows:

Achievement-oriented volunteers

◆ Ideal result of recognition is additional training or more challenging tasks

◆ Subject for recognition is best linked to a very specific accomplishment

◆ Phrasing of recognition through 'Best', 'Most' awards

◆ Recognition decision should include 'Checkpoints' or 'Records'

◆ Recipient should be selected by co-workers.

Affiliation-oriented volunteers

◆ Recognition should be given at a group event

◆ Recognition should be given in presence of peers, family, other bonded groupings

◆ Recognition item or award should have a personal touch

◆ Recognition should be organisational in nature, given by the organisation

◆ Recognition should be voted by peers

◆ If primary affiliative bonding is with a client rather than others in the organisation, then the client should take part in the recognition, through a personal note of thanks or as presenter of the award.

Power-oriented volunteers

◆ Key aspect of recognition is 'promotion, conveying greater access to authority or information'

◆ Recognition should be commendation from 'names'

◆ Recognition should be announced to community at large

◆ Recognition decision should be made by the organisation's leadership.

2 Style of volunteering

Recognition might also vary between long-term and short-term volunteers.

Long-term volunteer

◆ Recognition with and by the group

◆ Recognition entails greater power, involvement, information about the organisation

◆ Presenter of recognition is a person in authority

Short-term volunteer

◆ Recognition is given in immediate work unit or social group

◆ Recognition is portable; something which the volunteer can take with them when they leave – a present, photograph or other memorabilia of experience, training, and so on

◆ Recognition is provided via home or work – letter to employer, church or family

◆ Presenter is either the immediate supervisor or the client.

Day-to-day recognition may include such items as:

◆ saying 'thank you';

◆ involving the volunteer in decisions that affect them;

◆ asking about the volunteer's family and showing an interest in their 'outside' life;

◆ making sure that volunteers receive equal treatment to that given staff;

◆ sending a note of appreciation to the volunteer's family;

◆ allowing the volunteer to increase their skills by attending training;

◆ recommending the volunteer for promotion to a more responsible job;

◆ celebrating the volunteer's anniversary with the organisation.

You should note that an ideal recognition system might require a mixture of different procedures in order to have something for every type of volunteer. This is not unusual and is quite appropriate. Many organisations fail to do this, with interesting results. Consider, for example, an all-too-typical organisation that gives its volunteer awards only according to the amount of time donated, a 'longevity' prize. If you're a short-term volunteer how do you feel about this system? Or if your busy schedule limits the time you can offer? Could you ever win under these rules? What would this type of award suggest to you about the value that the organisation places upon your own contribution?

Recognising and rewarding volunteers

The following is taken from The British Trust for Conservation Volunteers' Guide to Working Practice

BTCV has always acknowledged the valuable contribution that volunteers make and that volunteers are an integral part of the organisation. This guide sets out BTCV's procedures and practice of working with volunteers to ensure that we continue to welcome all volunteers and that they have an enjoyable and successful time with us.

1.8 Retaining Volunteers

BTCV cares about its volunteers, wants them to enjoy their experience with the organisation and, as well as continuing to volunteer, to tell other people about that experience. The most common way volunteers hear about BTCV is by word of mouth so it is in our interest to help current volunteers spread the word. Below are some of the things that can help.

1.8.1 Natural Breaks postcards

Postcards are available for volunteers on Natural Breaks to send to their friends and relatives telling them about their holiday. They are sent to the local office with the volunteer list for each Natural Break and should be put into the leaders pack for the leader to give to the volunteers on the Break.

1.8.2. Socials

Social events for all volunteers in one geographical area are a great way of giving hard working volunteers the chance to relax and, by inviting them to bring a friend, introducing potential new volunteers. Talks, slide shows, barbecues, meals, bowling, quiz nights, are all possibles.

1.8.3. Visits

In a similar way visits to local places of interest can be a thank you to existing volunteers and a chance to invite new ones.

1.8.4. Volunteers week

This is organised every year by the National Centre for Volunteering who invite voluntary organisations to find some way of saying 'thank you' to their volunteers during the week. BTCV tries to say 'thank you' more than once a year but you may like to use the week as a focus for a particular event.

Ideas for recognition

Here are some examples of different levels of recognition activity.

Daily means of providing recognition:

◆ saying 'Thank you'

◆ telling them they did a good job

◆ suggesting they join you for coffee

◆ asking for their opinions

◆ greeting them when they come in the morning

◆ showing interest in their personal interests

◆ smiling when you see them

◆ bragging about them to your boss (in their presence)

◆ jotting small thank you notes to them

◆ having a drink with them after work

◆ saying something positive about their personal qualities.

Intermediate means of providing recognition:

◆ taking them to lunch

◆ providing food at volunteer meetings

◆ letting them put their names on the products they produce

◆ buying the first round of beer for 'the best crew of the month'

◆ writing them a letter of commendation (with copies to personnel file and other appropriate people)

◆ getting a local radio station to mention them

◆ putting them on important task forces or committees

◆ giving the best parking space to the 'employee of the month'

◆ posting graphic displays, showing progress toward targets

◆ mentioning major contributors by name in your status reports to upper management

◆ having them present their results to higher-ups

◆ giving permission to go to a seminar, convention, or professional meeting, if possible at the organisation's expense

◆ writing articles about their performance for newsletters or newspapers

- having them present a training session to co-workers
- decorating their work area on their birthday
- having your boss write them a letter of thanks
- celebrating major accomplishments
- having them represent you at important meetings
- putting their picture on the bulletin board with news of their accomplishments
- cutting out articles and cartoons they might be interested in
- organising informal chats with organisation leadership.

Major means of providing recognition:

- making special caps, shirts, belt buckles or lapel badges honouring the group
- encouraging them to write an article about some accomplishment at work
- giving a plaque, certificate, or trophy for being best employee, best crew, most improved results, and so on
- offering tuition assistance
- buying them good equipment
- getting their picture in the paper for outstanding accomplishment
- giving additional responsibilities and a new job title
- renting newspaper space to thank them
- putting up a banner celebrating a major accomplishment
- honouring them for years of service to the organisation
- giving them a bigger office
- enlisting them in training staff and other volunteers
- involving them in the annual planning process.

Rules for recognition

Whatever mix of recognition system you use, remember the following rules:

1   Give it or else.

The need for recognition is very important to most people. If volunteers don't get recognition for productive participation, only bad things can happen. The least of these is that they will feel unappreciated and drop out. Alternatively, they may start getting recognition from their peers (in the form of attention, laughter, camaraderie) for snide remarks and other, more serious disruptive behaviour.

2   Give it frequently.

The most common complaint of volunteers is that they don't get enough recognition from staff. Staff are usually surprised by this and can often cite examples in which they have given recognition to volunteers. The reason for this discrepancy of perception is that recognition has a short shelf-life. Its effects start to wear off after a few days, and after several weeks of not hearing anything positive, volunteers start to wonder if they are appreciated. Giving recognition once a year to a volunteer at a recognition banquet is certainly not enough.

3   It must be varied.

One of the implications of the previous rule is that you need a variety of methods of showing appreciation to volunteers. Fortunately, there are hundreds of methods. Recognition can be categorised into four major types:

◆ *For work the volunteer did (recognition from an individual).*

Examples include saying 'You did a great job on this' or writing them a letter to that effect.

◆ *For being part of the organisation (recognition from an individual).*

Examples include birthday celebrations or personal compliments such as 'I'm impressed by your pleasant attitude'. These have nothing to do with the volunteer's work performance and are expressions of appreciation of them as a person.

◆ *For work the volunteer did (recognition from the organisation).*

Examples would include a plaque commemorating their work on a project or being honoured as 'Volunteer of the month' because of their outstanding achievements.

◆ *For being part of the team (recognition from the organisation).*

Examples include a plaque commemorating years of service or being featured in a newsletter article that tells interesting personal facts about the volunteer but is not written due to particular job performance.

All of these types are valid. Some appeal more to people than to others.

4 It must be honest.

Don't give praise unless you mean it. If you praise substandard performance, the praise you give to others for good work will not be valued. If a volunteer is performing poorly, you might be able to give them honest recognition for their effort or for some personality trait.

5 It should be given to the person, not to the work.

This is a subtle but important distinction. If volunteers organise a fund-raising event, for example, and you praise the event, the volunteers may feel some resentment. Make sure you connect the volunteer's name to it. It is better to say 'John, Betty, and Megan did a great job of organising this event', than to say 'This event was really well organised'.

6 It should be appropriate to the achievement.

Small accomplishments should be praised with low-effort methods, large accomplishments should get something more. For example, if a volunteer tutor teaches a child to spell 'cat', we could say 'well done!'. If they write an application that doubles our funding, a banner lauding their accomplishments might be more appropriate.

7 It should be consistent.

If two volunteers are responsible for similar achievements, they ought to get similar recognition. If one gets their picture in the entrance hall and another gets an approving nod, the latter may feel resentment. This does not mean that the recognition has to be exactly the same, but that it should be the result of similar effort on your part. Otherwise certain volunteers will come to be regarded as favourites, a stigma they may come to dread.

8 It must be timely.

Praise for work should come as soon as possible after the achievement. Don't save up your recognition for the annual banquet. If a volunteer has to wait months before hearing any word of praise, they may develop resentment for lack of praise in the meantime.

9 It should be individualised as much as possible.

Different people like different things. One might respond favourably to football tickets, another might find them useless. In order to provide effective recognition, you need to get to know your people and what they will respond to positively.

10 Pay attention to what you want more of.

Too often your staff pay most attention to volunteers who are having difficulty. Unfortunately, this may result in ignoring good performers. We are not suggesting that you ignore below-par volunteers, just that you make sure that you praise the efforts of those who are doing a good job.

If all else fails, do things correctly

The final answer to volunteer retention and recognition is quite simple – operate a well-managed programme. Volunteers, like the rest of us, tend to make rational decisions about the allocation of their time; they will strive to spend it in settings where they feel valued. This value may be the social aspects, the work objectives, the situational settings, or a combination of all of these. Programmes that can give volunteers a work setting in which they can do good work, in a good setting, with good people are uniquely positioned to provide this sense of value and accomplishment, and often can do so in ways that paid work settings are not able to provide. The principles of good volunteer management described in other chapters outline the actions which can enable a volunteer programme to provide this positive environment. Always remember McCurley's Law of Volunteer Retention:

'The longer a volunteer is around the more likely they are to notice when the elements of good volunteer management are not in place. The honeymoon is over.'

CHAPTER TEN

Volunteer-staff Relations

Good volunteer-staff relations are critical to all organisations, and of particular concern when you are introducing volunteers into an organisation or project for the first time. This chapter outlines the concerns that staff may have about volunteer involvement and ways to ensure that volunteer-staff relations are both happy and productive.

THINKING ABOUT VOLUNTEERS FROM THE STAFF'S PERSPECTIVE

Imagine for a moment that you are a staff member who has never worked with a computer. At a staff meeting the director of your organisation announces that computerisation is the only answer to the enormous workload that your organisation faces, and that they intend to obtain as much computer equipment as they can for staff, none of whom at this point are computer literate. They announce that have just hired a Director of Computer Operations to get the organisation moving on this.

Topics covered include:

- **The role of the volunteer manager**

- **Dealing with staff concerns**

- **An eight-part system for good volunteer-staff relations**

- **An important role for senior management**

- **The need to create an organisational climate that recognises and respects volunteer usage**

Shortly after this meeting, the new Director of Computer Operations walks into your office, deposits a computer on your desk, says "Here's your new computer, hope you enjoy it!", and walks out. There is no instruction manual, no training session, you have no knowledge of how to operate the machine, and little space in your office to accommodate it.

What would you do in this situation?
- bang at the keys until something happened?
- place the computer in the corner and use it as a plant stand?

◆ How would you feel if you were the staff person, given a possible resource that you don't fully understand and may even resent for the changes it imposes on your work style?

It may sound strange, but volunteers and computers have a lot in common: each resource has suffered from haphazard attempts to implement its use within voluntary organisations and each resource is complicated and multi-faceted. Each requires specific skills on the part of the staff who will be using it. And each, to be most effective, needs to be customised for the particular usages, setting, and personalities involved.

About the only differences between a computer and a volunteer, from a strictly management view, are that volunteers are more complex (they can do a greater variety of things, if operated properly) and they are less forgiving. A volunteer, for example, doesn't take kindly to being asked to stand in the corner and serve as a plant stand until needed.

This is a round-about way of explaining that staff difficulties in working with volunteers – whether these include active opposition, passive resistance, or simple inability to achieve creative usage – are probably not the fault of the staff.

For the most part, staff who are being encouraged to make use of volunteers are in an equivalent position to a person being given a computer and told: 'bang the keys until something happens'. No matter how well-meaning the member of staff is, they are unlikely to accomplish much. They are likely to become frustrated. And, most importantly, they are highly likely to damage the equipment.

CHANGING PATTERNS OF VOLUNTEER USE

To understand why this inability to work with volunteers is so damaging, we must realise the immense changes that have taken place in volunteer involvement patterns during the past decade. (See diagrams left and opposite.)

Visually, one could represent the management relationships involved in this system as a simple, two-sided continuum

Volunteers ⟷ Volunteer Manager

Twenty years ago most volunteer departments operated, for the most part, on their own, and a volunteer coordinator (either paid or unpaid) supervised the activities of volunteers engaged in a variety of projects or activities.

Usually these volunteers were engaged in programme activities that were somewhat separate from the other organisational operations. The volunteer coordinator was responsible for almost all recruitment, job development, and supervision of volunteers. In some cases this could result in rather strange management systems where one volunteer coordinator was supposed to be in charge of hundreds or even thousands of volunteers.

"A volunteer, for example, doesn't take well to being asked to stand in the corner and serve as a plant stand until needed".

As volunteer involvement has become more sophisticated, this situation has changed considerably. Volunteers have diffused throughout the structure of an organisation, become a more integral part of it, and sometimes assumed tasks and responsibilities that had previously been done by paid staff. As new activities are undertaken by the volunteers, they begin to work more in partnership with staff, operating as aides or members of teams, or simply as assigned workers to a staff department. They begin to work regularly with and for other members of staff than the volunteer coordinator. In some cases they are totally seconded to other staff.

This new system of volunteers working more directly with individual staff has totally changed the dynamics of effective volunteer management.

This new three-sided relationship is much more complex than the two-sided continuum. There are two major differences which this new system creates.

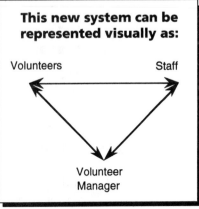

This new system can be represented visually as:

- ◆ A requirement that the volunteer manager view their job in a quite different fashion. As you can see from the connective lines of the triangle, the volunteer director 'links' both to volunteers and to staff. This means that work must be done with both to be successful.

- ◆ A realisation that the line relationship between the staff and the volunteers is the primary line of management and supervision. If volunteers work on a day-to-day basis with staff, whether through an assignment with a single staff member, or in conjunction with several staff, then it is the quality of that management and interpersonal interaction which will determine whether the volunteer is effectively and satisfactorily involved.

The operational relationships will vary in different organisations. Generally, the larger the organisation the more likely it is that volunteers will be working more directly with staff. It is quite apparent, however, that this new system is the most effective method of getting the most out of volunteers and staff.

Think back to the computer example. If a staff member is provided with a computer, does the Director of Computer Operations attempt to operate the keyboard for each person? Obviously not; indeed, the idea is ridiculous. Why, then, should we not also expect staff to 'operate' the volunteers with whom they work?

For volunteer use to be effective, each staff member must understand and be able to implement volunteer management. They must have the capacity to comprehend the diversity of the volunteer workforce, to create imaginative and meaningful jobs for volunteers, and to effectively lead and supervise those volunteers with whom they work.

They must become, in essence, *'Managers of Volunteers'*.

New roles for the volunteer manager

Volunteer managers must realise that preparing staff for these new responsibilities may necessitate a change in their own role. One way of explaining this shift is to simply note the subtle but significant difference between two phrases:

Manager of Volunteers
Manager of Volunteer Services

The first implies a person who manages volunteers. This is the person responsible for everyday management and supervision of individual volunteers. Sticking with our computer analogy, the equivalent phrase would be Computer Operator.

The second indicates the person who is responsible for overall operations involving volunteers, but who does not manage each individual volunteer. Instead they enable, assist, and prepare each member of staff to make effective use of their own volunteers. In the computer analogy this would be the Director of Computer Operations.

What is needed is for volunteer managers to take a broader interpretation of their roles, viewing themselves as being responsible for the system of volunteer involvement within the organisation, which includes working closely with both volunteers and staff.

Alas, in the real world this process is made somewhat more difficult. Quite often volunteer managers lack the real or apparent authority to direct anyone, much less senior organisation staff.

This lack of power makes it necessary for the successful volunteer manager to approach the role somewhat differently, assuming the guise of a consultant, one who helps when needed and one who does not, and usually cannot, order anyone to do anything.

The consultant, in a situation of this sort, engages in two types of teaching behaviour.

◆ The first is *diagnosis*. In this context that means working with staff, sometimes on an individual basis, to help identify the ways in which volunteers can assist them in accomplishing the work within their purview. The key element in this process lies in showing staff how to think about volunteers in such a way that they can continue to think of appropriate and creative usages for volunteers.

◆ The second is *instruction*. This would involve educating staff about the requirements and techniques of working effectively with volunteers. In essence, the volunteer manager turns the staff into 'volunteer operators', knowledgeable about both the overall system of volunteer involvement in the organisation and supervision of individual volunteers.

The volunteer manager will then identify, recommend and implement all the organisational actions which are needed to make it possible for staff to successfully accomplish the tasks and activities identified during the diagnosis and instructional phase.

In all of this, the volunteer manager, acting as a consultant, concentrates on working with staff, not in attempting to coerce them. The point is to persuade and empower staff to think about volunteers from the perspective of a trained 'volunteer manager'.

And, much as knowledge of, and even affection for, computers has blossomed among staff, so you can succeed in inculcating the same improvement in relationships between staff and volunteers.

Dealing with staff concerns

"Volunteer time is discretionary time, and most people prefer to spend their discretionary time in a pleasant environment".

A good volunteer manager will begin by recognising that staff may have legitimate fears or concerns about the use of volunteers. The role of the volunteer manager is to identify these concerns and then transform them into a sense of confidence among the staff that the volunteers will be a useful addition to the organisation.

In general, this means imparting two feelings to staff:

1 a sense of benefits greater than the difficulties or problems;

2 a feeling of control over the situation.

Staff concerns may be:

◆ a fear of loss of control

◆ a fear of diminished quality of service

◆ a fear that volunteers will be unreliable

◆ a fear of increased legal problems.

◆ a resentment of increased work load

◆ a fear of loss of a job

◆ a fear of having to manage volunteers without experience to do so.

Staff are more likely to be satisfied with the volunteers they will be working with if they perceive that the return to them is greater than the effort involved, and if they believe that they will be closely involved in making decisions that affect how they are to work with the volunteers.

In dealing with staff concerns, it is wise to note that your natural instincts (to 'fight and win') may be disastrous. Many volunteer managers attempt to deal with staff concerns by throwing their weight around, often seeking a top management mandate that 'volunteers *will* be assigned to all staff'.

This approach is fatal. It will leave the staff unhappy, and feeling that another's will has been imposed upon them. More importantly, they will probably vent their frustrations upon the only available target – the volunteers.

Such a situation can also involve you in unpleasant political games. These affect the morale of the organisation in adverse ways. In cases where there is a lot of conflict among staff, or where there is a bad atmosphere, volunteer turnover will be high. If a volunteer senses tension and conflict in the organisation, they will be deterred from continuing to work. They are giving their time to you on a discretionary basis, and most people prefer to spend their discretionary time in a pleasant environment.

Another fatal approach is the use of criticism. Arguing with staff is futile; telling them five reasons why they are wrong is futile. Many staff concerns will not be built entirely upon logic, and, indeed, may not even be directly related to the volunteer programme. Directly confronting staff may only produce a defensiveness that will turn to hostility if you continue to push the issue.

CREATING A SYSTEM OF GOOD VOLUNTEER-STAFF RELATIONS

A system for good volunteer-staff relations requires that the following eight elements be in place.

1 Overall policy on volunteer use

The organisation should have an overall policy on volunteer use, expressing why the organisation employs volunteers.

Reasons may include:

◆ provide community outreach and input

◆ gain additional human resources

◆ cost savings

◆ supplement expertise of staff

◆ allow involvement of client groups

◆ demonstrate community support

◆ act as conduit to funders

◆ provide personal touch in services to clients.

The policy should provide a clear rationale, which can be used in explaining the volunteer programme both to staff and to potential volunteers. It indicates to the staff that the volunteer programme is not just an emergency measure dreamed up one weekend by a desperate Executive Director, but is one which fits within the overall mission of the organisation. The policy should:

◆ be adopted and supported by trustees and other top policy makers;

◆ be integrated into overall organisation plans and budgets;

◆ encourage, but not mandate, staff involvement.

This last point is often overlooked, but is crucial. It is impossible to force staff to work effectively with volunteers. There are too many ways for staff to sabotage volunteer effort to think that staff can ever be coerced into productively using volunteers when they do not want to. Even indifference of staff will quickly communicate itself to volunteers, who will equally quickly decide not to be where they are not wanted. Mandatory policies create resistance, and you will only be asking for trouble if you attempt to force compliance. Plan to work through rewards for productive staff, not punishments.

Dealing with staff concerns

The National Trust produces the following guidelines for volunteer managers on dealing with volunteer–staff relations.

Introduction

Unless members of staff have personal experience of volunteering, they may be unsure about working with people who are not paid, and may fear or even resent the involvement of volunteers.

Their concerns may be that volunteers will:

◆ be a threat to their job

◆ increase their workload

◆ take over an aspect of their work they themselves enjoy

◆ result in a loss of control or lower standards

◆ be less conscientious or unreliable

◆ require them to act as supervisors.

These fears are real to the individual and managers need to give staff reassurance about their roles and abilities, and to stress the benefits volunteers can bring to a project.

Best Practice

◆ Avoid building unnecessary resentment by keeping staff informed if it is planned to bring in additional volunteer help, especially those members of staff with whom the volunteer must work closely.

◆ Involve staff in the selection process and ask their views on the kind of help they need and the qualities they would look for. Introduce prospective volunteers to the office and get feedback from the staff.

◆ The Trust's volunteers complement and add to the work done by Trust staff, but are not a substitute.

◆ For some staff, this may be the first occasion that they have been expected to supervise the work of others. This should be presented as a way to add to their abilities before they see it as adding stress. The Trust runs courses at two levels in supervising others, as well as the Working with Volunteers courses which can be run for all staff at a property if requested.

◆ The standard of work is set by managers and there is no reason to assume that a volunteer would be any less conscientious than a paid employee.

You might also want to make sure that staff understand the need for volunteers, and that the volunteers are being involved to help, not hinder, staff.

Such a communication (see above) can pro-actively address staff concerns and smooth the way for a successful staff-volunteer relationship.

2 An assessment of staff capabilities

The more you know about your staff, the better you can design a system which takes into account their individual characteristics and needs. A very effective preliminary tool is a quick survey of staff attitudes and experience with volunteers. This should ascertain the following:

Previous staff experience with volunteering.
This includes their own experience as volunteers, their previous work in an organisation which used volunteers, and any previous experience in supervising volunteers.

Staff attitudes towards the use of volunteers.
This would include the opinions of staff about the perceived need for volunteers, and any fears or recommendations about what jobs would be appropriate or inappropriate for volunteers. It would also include staff perceptions of what needs to happen before volunteers are brought into the organisation.

3 Staff orientation to the volunteer programme

Staff need to learn the system for volunteer involvement within the organisation. This would include an explanation of:

◆ rationale for using volunteers
◆ brief history of volunteer programme
◆ types of volunteers and the jobs they do
◆ the contributions volunteers can make
◆ the role of the staff in all aspects of working with volunteers.

This orientation might actually be provided in different ways and at different times. Part might be given to each new staff member. Part might be given as staff begin to be involved with volunteers. It may be given in a formal or informal setting, either in a workshop or one-on-one. It is very effective to include successful managers of volunteers and volunteers themselves as co-presenters during these sessions.

Some information may be provided in writing, as the example overleaf from the Oregon Department of Human Service brochure illustrates.

4 Personalised volunteer job creation

Ultimately, volunteer retention lies in having jobs which are interesting and rewarding, and that volunteers really enjoy doing. No recruitment campaign can compensate for boring volunteer

Case study

FROM THE OREGON DEPT OF HUMAN SERVICE

Can the volunteer programme help clients I can't help?

Helping people is what our organisations are all about. The Volunteer Programme can be a place to turn when you are unable to help a client. Sometimes volunteers will be able to meet some of the client's needs or assist you in identifying resources in the community. The Volunteer Programme can make the tough part of your job just a little easier.

What happens when you make a referral?

When you make a volunteer request, the local Volunteer Programme Supervisor's (VPS) response will depend on the type of request. If the help you need is available immediately, the request will be filled quickly. If the service, volunteer or resource isn't available, the Volunteer Programme will try to recruit, interview and register volunteers for you, or they may help you locate and access other resources. If the request is inappropriate for volunteer involvement, the VPS will call you to discuss available alternatives. Since the Volunteer Programme serves four different divisions (Adult and Family Services Division, Children's Services Division, Mental Health Division, and Senior Services Division) every effort will be made to provide equal access to the services available. Priorities for your Volunteer Programme are established by a local Volunteer Programme board, with representatives from each organisation.

How hard can it be to find lots of volunteers?

Our Volunteer Programme is competing with dozens of organisations in the recruitment of volunteers. Also, we're choosy; we want only the best. We screen all volunteer applicants to make sure they are appropriate and capable of serving our clients. Your help is important in keeping and attracting volunteers. Meaningful opportunities and positive experiences will keep present volunteers involved in our programme. Also those same opportunities and experiences will help us find new volunteers. Nothing attracts like success. We welcome your help. If you would like to register as a volunteer or know of someone else who would be interested, talk to your nearest Volunteer Programme. Our recruitment process is ongoing.

What does it take to get a volunteer going on a project?

Volunteers come to us with a vast range of abilities, experiences, and interests. Some may be well equipped for the jobs and others may require some training. Every volunteer you work with will need clear instructions in order to do the best job for you. The effort you spend training a volunteer and outlining clear performance expectations will make the experience positive and productive for both of you.

Also, since most volunteers have lots of other commitments, working out a mutually agreeable schedule is very important for both of you. Good planning helps ensure success for everyone, and encourages the volunteer to consider future projects that you may have.

jobs. This means that there needs to be a process in place for creating jobs which are meaningful to the member of staff who will be working with the volunteer (i.e. they really help out) and meaningful to potential volunteers. This process will work in three ways.

1. Providing staff with ideas prior to volunteer use

You might, for example, produce a guide for staff explaining what volunteers could contribute, which then starts them thinking about the various possibilities.

You could explain the different ways in which volunteers might help.

◆ Are there jobs that staff don't want to do? This may be because they are not skilled in that type of work, or are too skilled for the work, or else simply have a preference to concentrate their efforts on something else.

◆ Are there areas in which there is too much work for staff to do alone, and for which you might create volunteer assistants to supplement staff resources? These assistants might work directly with one member of staff or could do tasks that benefit all staff.

◆ Are there areas in which you can extend services because volunteers would enable the organisation to begin work that you cannot at present even consider undertaking?

You might also suggest the creation of volunteer jobs based on the recipients of the service. Consider the following:

◆ jobs that are of direct assistance to an individual client (counselling, visiting, buddying, mentoring, etc.);

◆ office administrative help (information services, filing, messengers, etc.);

◆ direct assistance to staff (research, training, computer help, etc.);

◆ outreach (speakers panel, fundraising, marketing and evaluation, research, etc.).

You might also want to suggest considerations that staff should bear in mind as they think about potential jobs, such as:

◆ the work must be meaningful and significant, both to the organisation and to the clientele;

◆ the work must be needed and should be interesting to the person doing it (this means that each volunteer job must have a goal or a purpose that the volunteer can accomplish and can feel good about having achieved);

◆ the volunteer ought to be able to feel some ownership and responsibility for the job. Volunteers like to feel that they have some input into and control over the work they are asked to do. This will mean including them in the flow of information and decision-making within the office;

◆ the work must fit a part-time situation (for a part-time volunteer). Either the work must be small enough in scope to be done in a few hours a week, or else it must be designed to be shared among a group of volunteers;

◆ volunteers must be worked with. They should be assigned to work with staff who are capable of supervising their activities in a productive fashion, and of providing on-going direction, evaluation and feedback.

Helping staff develop innovative jobs

The job development process is never-ending. New ideas should be continuously provided to staff. Among the ways to do this are:

1 Talent advertising:
disseminating information about volunteers who have recently joined the organisation with particular skills or expertise.

2 Success stories:
highlighting examples of innovative usage of volunteers, often best done by showing the success that staff have had in achieving some new goal or solving some problem through the involvement of volunteers.

3 Job upgrading:
organising scheduled evaluation sessions of volunteers to re-examine assignments and re-shape the job to take into account the growth and development of the volunteer.

The more flexible the timeframe of the volunteer job, the greater the likelihood that there will be someone willing to undertake it. Think about the following as different options for the job:

◆ can the work be done to a totally flexible schedule at the discretion of the volunteer?
◆ are there set hours during the week when the volunteer is needed?
◆ could the work be done in the evenings or at weekends?
◆ must the work be done on-site or at the office?

Assisting staff in creating volunteer jobs

The best method to assist staff in developing volunteer jobs is for the volunteer manager to interview each member of staff. The purpose of this interview is to match what the staff know about their work situation with what the volunteer manager knows about volunteers.

The following questions will generate ideas about possible tasks that volunteers might perform.

◆ What are the types of things you are in charge of? What kinds of things do you do to accomplish this work?
◆ What parts of your job do you really like to do?
◆ What parts of your job do you not like to do?
◆ What kind of knowledge or training would a person need to do this job?
◆ What would you do if you had a full-time staff person assigned as your assistant?
◆ What are the things that you would like to get done, that you never have time to do?
◆ Is there anything that you've always wanted to learn how to do?
◆ Is it possible volunteers might be able to do some of the things you do by working under your supervision?

It is also important to ask questions that will help with other parts of the volunteer involvement process:

◆ How might you ensure that the volunteers have the necessary training or knowledge?
◆ Are there any changes in the way you work that you will need to make in order to use volunteers?
◆ What changes in office operations should be made for volunteers to work here?

◆ What resources will you need in order for you to work with volunteers?

◆ What types of people do you prefer to work with?

◆ What types of people do you prefer not to work with?

While time-consuming, this interviewing process is by far the most productive method for developing ideas for meaningful and significant volunteer jobs, as well as providing the volunteer manager with vital information about matching and preparing volunteers. Chapter Four contains more information on how to assist staff in developing volunteer jobs.

5 Early monitoring of volunteer placements

Those staff who are afraid of a loss of quality control will be made more comfortable if they are included in the selection and induction process. Allow staff to help develop the criteria by which volunteers will be chosen, to participate in interviewing potential volunteers for their department, and to design and present portions of the volunteer training sessions.

Initial assignments for the volunteer can be on a trial basis. It is a bit irrational to assume following a 30-minute interview that you know precisely where this volunteer will be most effective. It is far better to give a temporary assignment, with a review after 30 days. During this period, the volunteer can sample the job and the organisation, and determine if it matches their needs. The staff member who works with the volunteer can also see if the volunteer has the qualifications and commitment required for the job. The volunteer manager can see that the volunteer and the member of staff have those elements that are essential to a mutually productive working relationship. The experience of this initial trial period can then be used to finalise the placement of the volunteer. If changes need to made, then it is much better to do them at this early stage than to wait until disaster strikes.

You will also need to monitor the staff providing training for the volunteer.

6 Staff control and responsibility in volunteer management

Once staff become accustomed to the idea of supervising 'their' volunteers, the majority will be happy to accept this responsibility. The role of the volunteer manager is to teach them how to do this correctly, particularly insofar as managing volunteers is different from managing paid staff, and to assist them in dealing with problem situations.

Case Study

FROM CATHOLIC CHARITIES OF THE ARCHDIOCESE OF ST PAUL AND MINNEAPOLIS

Minimum standards for supervisors of volunteers

We ask the volunteer supervisor to:

1 Attend required volunteer supervisor orientation/training.

2 Work with volunteer coordinator to clearly define volunteer positions which the supervisor is requesting (including duties, qualifications, and time commitment to fulfil the position). Keep volunteer coordinator informed of changes in job description.

3 Participate with the volunteer coordinator in the selection of volunteers for the specific position.

4 Provide specific on-site orientation and training for volunteers.

5 Assure regular contact with volunteers for whom you are responsible, and provide a minimum of annual formal evaluation session.

6 Communicate key information to volunteers which will affect the volunteer's performance (i.e. current operating information, changes in schedules, training, meeting dates, and changes in client status).

7 Assure report of volunteer's hours/impact to the volunteer coordinator.

8 Participate in formal and informal volunteer recognition activities.

9 Notify the volunteer coordinator of any problems or questions regarding a volunteer as soon as they become evident and prior to any decision to terminate.

10 Advise the volunteer coordinator when a volunteer terminates and/or has a change in volunteer status.

Supervisors of volunteers exceed expectations by:

1 Attending additional training regarding supervision.

2 Assisting the volunteer coordinator in recruitment of volunteers and being aware of organisational volunteer needs.

3 Designing and implementing the volunteer training and training materials.

4 Contributing to the volunteer's professional growth, including such things as resume writing, career laddering, reference letters, and special trainings.

5 Planning and implementing formal and informal recognition activities for volunteers.

6 Along with the volunteer coordinator, solving problems around potential issues/problems regarding volunteers and the volunteer programme.

7 Engaging with the volunteer coordinator in the annual planning process for the volunteer programme.

8 Participating in the divisional volunteer programme by serving on a task force or advisory committee.

Be sure that you clarify the web of relationships between the volunteer, the member of staff and the volunteer manager. The staff must understand whether supervision is being done by themselves or by the volunteer manager. They must understand who is in charge of what, who is responsible for what, and what should happen if things go wrong. Who, for example, is in charge of firing an unsatisfactory volunteer? The member of staff ? The volunteer manager? Is it a unilateral decision or a joint one? Is there any appeal or grievance procedure?

Here are some specfic tips

Support the initial decision to employ volunteers:

◆ Attempt to reduce staff anxiety by indicating that the decision is under their control at all times.
◆ Follow-up, both by telephone and face-to-face, to discuss potential problems.
◆ Ask for feedback, both positive and negative.
◆ Introduce staff to other volunteer users. Build a support network.

Help manage the implementation:

◆ Keep in touch, and keep staff informed on progress or lack of it.
◆ Assist staff with getting the decision to use volunteers approved.
◆ Assist staff with paperwork.
◆ Involve staff in recruitment, interviewing, induction, etc.
◆ Advise staff of key management requirements.

Deal with dissatisfaction:

◆ Empathise with staff feelings.
◆ Respond to problems promptly.
◆ Continue to anticipate concerns and expectations.
◆ Reinforce the anticipated benefits.
◆ Never attempt to force continuing use of volunteers if things are not working out - withdraw the volunteers and deal with problem, then seek to re-introduce usage.

Enhance the relationship:

◆ Be available.
◆ Arrange for continual personal communication.
◆ Do not wait for staff to come to you - check for problems and approach them.
◆ Facilitate open, candid communication.
◆ Maintain high quality volunteer referrals.
◆ Become a resource for information, help, new ideas, problem solving.
◆ Praise staff for good work, and inform their line manager.

The extent of staff involvement will vary, depending upon the particular member of staff's own comfort and desire for management responsibilities. Even if the volunteer manager still controls and supervises the volunteer, an effort should be made to make the member of staff feel a part of the supervisory team and to keep him or her informed about what is happening. You can do this by asking their advice about how the volunteer should be treated, or inquiring as to how they think the volunteer is doing at the job. The organisation might also create set standards for staff supervison of volunteers.

7 Feedback and recognition

The final element in a system for staff involvement is continuing to demand more volunteer help. This includes:

◆ providing managerial information to staff on quantities and patterns of volunteer use;

◆ showing examples of successful and innovative use of volunteers;

◆ implementing rewards and recognition for successful staff managers of volunteers.

Rewards for staff may range from formal recognition of their accomplishment to increased chances for promotion, and some informal recognition of their skills (represented by their inclusion in volunteer management activities, training, staff orientations, and so on).

8 On-going relationship building

What you are trying to create is an overall organisational climate that recognises and respects volunteer usage. This means that true recognition should occur throughout the management process. Including volunteer use in overall evaluations of the organisation's accomplishments, or evaluating staff in their proficiency in volunteer supervision, are much more meaningful indicators than certificates handed to staff on an annual basis, and staff will be well aware of the difference.

SENIOR MANAGEMENT SUPPORT

Senior management must not only endorse the use of volunteers in the organisation but also the overall concept of a volunteer programme.

Keys to management support

There are three elements which are essential in gaining support from senior management.

1 _Understanding_

Senior management must understand the volunteer programme in terms of what it aims to achieve and how it operates, including the relationship of the volunteers to the staff.

2 _Information_

Senior management must understand what the volunteer programme can accomplish compared with the financial and personnel costs required to run the programme, and must understand that the benefits outweigh the costs.

3 _Involvement_

Senior management must understand what they can and should do to assist the volunteer programme.

Understanding

Obtaining a firm commitment from senior management first requires that they actually understand the nature of the volunteer programme.

This requires that they themselves know why they wish to have volunteers connected with the organisation. Senior management must be happy with their decision to introduce a volunteer programme, and recognise that the volunteers have the ability to contribute to the success of the organisation.

Their decision should be based on whatever rationale they choose to adopt, whether viewing volunteers as a source of community input or community outreach, or simply viewing volunteers as a cost-effective service delivery. The particular rationale is not as important as the fact that there is _some_ commonly accepted reason for volunteer involvement. If there is not, you would be wise to lead senior staff through a planning exercise to formulate one. If you do not do this, you risk having several different, and perhaps mutually exclusive, opinions of why the volunteer programme should exist, or risk the prospect that no one in senior management really understands why it does exist. It is difficult to support something which you do not fully understand, particularly in a budget crisis.

Linked to this rationale is a second requirement, that senior management understand what needs to be done to have an effective volunteer programme. They must have an understanding of the volunteer management process and the investment needed to make effective use of volunteers.

Information

Senior management support will require sufficient information to judge whether the volunteer programme is successful.

This information can take a number of forms.

Patterns of volunteer use

This might consist of reports on where and how volunteers are being deployed. A report would include, for example, a department-by-department listing of how many volunteers are involved, how many hours they are contributing, and what types of jobs they are doing. The value of this type of report is that it allows senior management to identify patterns of usage, highlighting staff and departments who are doing a particularly good job of involving volunteers and those who are not.

It also shows senior management the types of work that volunteers are capable of doing.

Value of the volunteers

It is useful to include estimates of the value to the organisation of the volunteer contribution. This would include tracking a number of items.

◆ Value of donated volunteer time: calculating the number of volunteer hours and multiplying it by an estimated hourly wage. This estimated wage can be derived from a statistical estimate of what volunteers would otherwise earn with their time in their occupations, or by a calculated figure for each particular volunteer job (for example, a legal advisor would be valued at a much higher hourly rate than a general dogsbody).

◆ Value of in-kind donations by volunteers: recording the value of any personal or business equipment donated by the volunteer, including use of business office space or other facilities, personal equipment, and so on.

◆ Direct cash donations by volunteers: tracking any direct donations made by volunteers. Studies have shown that volunteers are much more likely than any other group to make a donation – although some organisations have a policy of not approaching their volunteers for cash support. Another measure might be legacy pledges.

◆ Non-reimbursed volunteer expenses: recording the expenses incurred by volunteers (mileage, phone calls, copying, etc.) for which they have not sought organisation reimbursement. Some organisations have a policy of encouraging reimbursement of all volunteer expenses, but then providing a system for the re-donation of such expenses back to the organisation.

Information should be provided to senior management in a combination of facts (statistics, lists) and stories (anecdotes, case studies, interesting personalities or snippets of information, and so on).

Involvement

The final element of senior management support involves telling them how and when they can be helpful to the programme.

There are several functions at which an appearance by senior management is extremely valuable. These include appearing at volunteer orientations, giving out volunteer recognition items, and meeting occasionally with groups of volunteers. It also includes being generally supportive on an on-going basis. One excellent example of top management support occurs in a hospital whose chief administrator has an hourly meeting with volunteers each Tuesday, rotating the invitees among the volunteers in various departments. Another hospital administrator memorises names and photographs of new volunteers, and then casually greets them in the halls of the hospital, welcoming them on behalf of the institution.

Senior managers also have a role to play in encouraging staff to value the volunteer input, to reward staff who work well with volunteers, and to convince other staff that they should work harder.

Key points

Follow these three general principles in planning your work with staff.

1 Try to spend at least as much time working with staff as you do working directly with your volunteers. In the initial development of your programme plan to spend much more time with the staff.

2 Deal with problems that arise as quickly as possible. Do not let a situation fester. And do not attempt to force people to get along. It is better for the volunteer to be transferred elsewhere than for you to try to enforce compatibility.

3 Your ultimate objective is to get the staff to do the core work of volunteer management. If you can enable staff to become effective volunteer managers then you will be able to spend your time working on creative job development and troubleshooting. If you are forced to attempt to supervise all of the volunteers in the organisation, then you will be overwhelmed by the trivial.

Perhaps the best encouragement that senior management can provide staff is through example. If the top management makes effective use of volunteers, other staff will get a clear message about the value and importance of volunteers to the organisation.

THE FUTURE

In an absolute sense, it is difficult to draw any clear philosophical distinction between what is inherently a staff function and what is a volunteer function. Different organisations will reach very different conclusions about appropriate patterns of work, based on philosophy, history, contractual agreements.

It is also difficult to contemplate some of the possible managerial implications for the more creative arrangements which are now being experimented with. In the US, for example, the American National Red Cross has been contemplating implications of their staffing patterns, which consist of paired teams of volunteers and staff at all levels, and in which volunteers exercise supervisory responsibility over paid staff. Overleaf are some of the resultant managerial recommendations from their *Volunteer 2000* report.

Case study

THE AMERICAN NATIONAL RED CROSS MANAGERIAL RECOMMENDATIONS

II-2 It is recommended that the degree of volunteer involvement in a unit or service not be measured by absolute increases or decreases in volunteer numbers, but rather by the degree of volunteer intensiveness, i.e., the ratio between volunteer and paid staff.

II-4 It is recommended that training in volunteer administration and/or substantial experience in volunteer administration be a prerequisite for being hired into a Red Cross human resources management position.

VI-4 It is recommended that where paid staff/volunteer teams exist, performance evaluation occur on team basis rather than one team member evaluating the other. The evaluation of team relationships should take place in one of two ways:

◆ the team is evaluated as a unit, and both partners share responsibility for the achievement of the entire spectrum of the unit's performance goals regardless of how they did, in fact, split the work load between them. In this method, the person or team at the next level reviews progress and adequacy of support levels with both team members simultaneously and in the presence of both;

◆ the partners are reviewed as individuals, each having negotiated separate performance goals and levels of support which, taken together, are the performance standards for the team. These performance and support goals for each partner would be negotiated initially between them, then in conference with the next higher level. The performance appraisal would be done by the next higher level.

VI-6 It is recommended that individual performance standards for paid and volunteer leadership staff always include as measures the degree of success demonstrated by that individual in recruiting and developing qualified volunteers for established volunteer positions, the degree of success in finding new ways of involving volunteers, and the degree of success in nominating appropriately qualified volunteers for awards and beyond-the-chapter positions.

These clearly envision a partnership in which the key factor is not that of who is paid and who is not, but rather how well the work is accomplished.

CHAPTER ELEVEN
Some Final Suggestions

FINDING AN OVERALL APPROACH

In tackling the work outlined in the previous chapters it is essential to employ a coherent philosophical approach. Our suggestion for this approach would have you concentrate on two theories, which we think will make success more probable.

Start small, and grow with success

Do not expect to accomplish everything at once, and do not try to do so. Operating a volunteer programme is a delicate and complicated task, made so in part by the fact that the more successful you are at some things (such as recruitment), then the more work you will create for yourself. It is better to begin with little things and then grow a bit at a time, than to become over-extended and create bad feelings with unsuccessful volunteer placements.

> ### The Golden Rule
>
> Remember the 'Golden Rule' of volunteer management:
>
> **Their niceness will let you recruit a volunteer the first time, but only your competence will let you keep them...**

Happy staff and volunteers will become the best promoters for your programme, but you have to make sure everyone is content.

One way to start small is to begin with an *ad hoc* effort, a programme intended to make use of volunteers to accomplish just one thing. This will allow you to test the use of volunteers and identify the strengths and weaknesses that the organisation brings to involving volunteers.

Rely on persuasion, not coercion

Do not try to force volunteers on the organisation or on any member of staff. The use of volunteers will help an organisation, but only if a positive approach is adopted. Rely on the persuasion that is created by competence and success – if staff realise that some departments are benefitting from the use of volunteers then eventually they will decide to seek the same advantages for themselves. Have confidence in the value of volunteers, and be willing to let staff come to you, rather than feeling compelled to beg them. Never be foolish enough to believe that you can coerce anyone into using volunteers. A well-operated, small volunteer programme is much more valuable then an ineffective large one.

Do not be afraid to make staff earn the right to have volunteers assigned to them. This will help to convince staff that volunteers are not a free resource, and will demonstrate that the organisation considers volunteers too valuable to be distributed to those who are not willing to make effective use of them.

THE GEOMETRY OF VOLUNTEER INVOLVEMENT

As you think about operating the programme, try to keep in mind the simple geometric shapes:

The Puzzle Square
representing the jobs which the organisation needs doing.

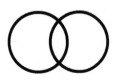

The Overlapping Circles
representing the commonly met needs of the organisation and the volunteers.

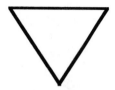

The Triangle
representing the web of relationships among the volunteer manager, the volunteer, and staff.

If you can construct a volunteer programme which embodies these three shapes, you will have created a mechanism for effectively using volunteer resources.

APPENDIX A
Sample Policy on Volunteer Management

This sample policy on volunteer management includes many of the ideas for good volunteer involvement expressed in this book. Not every item will be appropriate for every organisation, nor will the specific policy items suggested necessarily conform with how the organisation wishes to work with its volunteers. The sample policy is included more as a structure to help you construct your own policy on volunteer management which matches your views and needs, and which is appropriate to the size of your organisation and the ways in which you use your volunteers. To construct such a policy you may remove or amend any item, or even add further items not included here.

1. The volunteer programme

1.1 Overall policy on use of volunteers

The achievement of the goals of this organisation is best served by the active participation of citizens of the community. To this end, the organisation accepts and encourages the involvement of volunteers at all levels in the organisation and within all appropriate programmes and activities. All staff are encouraged to assist in the creation of meaningful and productive roles in which volunteers might serve and to assist in recruitment of volunteers from the community.

1.2 Purpose of the volunteer policy

The purpose of the policy is to provide overall guidance and direction to staff and volunteers engaged in volunteer involvement and management efforts. The policy is intended for internal management guidance only, and does not constitute, either implicitly or explicitly, a binding contractual or personnel agreement. The organisation reserves the exclusive right to change any aspect of the policy at any time and to expect adherence to the changed policy. Alterations to or exceptions from these policies may only be granted by the volunteer programme manager, and must be obtained in advance and in writing. Matters in areas not specifically covered by the policy shall be decided by the volunteer programme manager.

1.3 Scope of the volunteer policy

Unless specifically stated, the policy applies to all non-elected volunteers in all programmes and projects undertaken by or on behalf of the organisation, and to all departments and sites of operation of the organisation.

1.4 Role of the volunteer management department

The productive use of volunteers requires a planned and organised effort. The function of the volunteer management department is to provide a central coordinating point for effective volunteer management within the organisation, and to direct and assist staff and volunteer efforts jointly to provide more productive services. The department shall also bear responsibility for maintaining liaison with other volunteer programmes in the community and assisting in community-wide efforts to recognise and promote volunteering. The volunteer programme manager shall bear primary responsibility for planning for effective volunteer deployment, for assisting staff in identifying productive and creative volunteer roles, for recruiting suitable volunteers, and for tracking and evaluating the contribution of volunteers to the organisation.

1.5 Definition of 'volunteer'

A volunteer is anyone who without compensation or expectation of compensation beyond reimbursement of expenses incurred in the course of his or her volunteer duties, performs a task at the direction of and on behalf of the organisation. A volunteer must be officially accepted and enrolled by the organisation prior to performance of the task. Unless specifically stated, volunteers shall not be considered as employees of the organisation.

1.6 Special case volunteers

The organisation also accepts as volunteers those participating in student community service activities, student intern projects, alternative sentencing programmes, employee volunteering programmes, and other volunteer referral programmes. In each of these cases, however, a special agreement must be in effect with the agency, school, company, or programme from which the special case volunteers originate and must identify responsibility for management and care of the volunteers.

1.7 Employees as volunteers

The organisation accepts [*does not accept*] the services of its own staff as volunteers. This service is accepted provided that the volunteer service is provided totally without any coercive nature, involves work which is outside the scope of normal staff duties, and is provided outside usual working hours. Family members of staff are [*are not*] allowed to volunteer with the organisation. When family members are enrolled as volunteers, they will not be placed under the direct supervision or within the same department as other members of their family who are employees.

1.8 Clients and relatives as volunteers

Clients of the organisation may be accepted as volunteers, where such service does not constitute an obstruction to or conflict with provision of services to the client or to others. Relatives of clients may also serve as volunteers, but will not be placed in a position of direct service or relationship to members of their family who are receiving services.

1.9 Service at the discretion of the organisation

The organisation accepts the service of all volunteers with the understanding that such service is at the sole discretion of the organisation. Volunteers agree that the organisation may at any time, for whatever reason, decide to terminate the volunteer's relationship with the organisation.

A volunteer may at any time, for whatever reason, decide to sever their relationship with the organisation. Notice of such a decision should be communicated as soon as possible to the volunteer's supervisor.

1.10 Volunteer rights and responsibilities

Volunteers are viewed as a valuable resource to this organisation, its staff, and its clients. Volunteers shall be extended the right to be given meaningful assignments, the right to be treated as equal co-workers, the right to effective supervision, the right to full involvement and participation, and the right to recognition for work done. In return, volunteers shall agree to actively perform their duties to the best of their abilities and to remain loyal to the values, goals and procedures of the organisation.

1.11 Scope of volunteer involvement

Volunteers may be involved in all programmes and activities of the organisation, and serve at all levels of skill and decision-making. Volunteers should not, however, be used to displace any paid employees from their positions.

2. Volunteer management procedures

2.1 Maintenance of records

A system of records will be maintained on each volunteer, including dates of service, positions held, duties performed, evaluation of work, and awards received. Volunteers and appropriate staff shall be responsible for submitting all appropriate records and information to the volunteer management department in a timely and accurate fashion.

Volunteer personnel records shall be accorded the same confidentiality as staff personnel records.

2.2 Two hat policy

Members of the organisation's management committee are [are not] accepted as direct service volunteers with the organisation.

2.3 Conflict of interest

No person who has a conflict of interest with any activity or programme of the organisation, whether personal, philosophical, or financial shall be accepted or serve as a volunteer.

2.4 Representation of the organisation

Prior to any action or statement which might significantly affect or obligate the organisation, volunteers should seek prior consultation and approval from appropriate staff. These actions may include, but are not limited to, public statements to the press, lobbying efforts with other organisations, collaborations or joint initiatives, or any agreements involving contractual or other financial obligations. Volunteers are authorised to act as representatives of the organisation as specifically indicated within their job descriptions and only to the extent of such written specifications.

2.5 Confidentiality

Volunteers are responsible for maintaining the confidentiality of all proprietary or privileged information to which they are exposed while serving as a volunteer, whether this information involves a single member of staff, volunteer, client, or other person or involves the overall business of the organisation.

Failure to maintain confidentiality may result in termination of the volunteer's relationship with the organisation or other corrective action.

2.6 Worksite

An appropriate worksite shall be established prior to the enrolment of any volunteer. This worksite shall contain necessary facilities, equipment, and space to enable the volunteer to effectively and comfortably perform their duties.

2.7 Dress code

As representatives of the organisation, volunteers, like staff, are responsible for presenting a good image to clients and to the community. Volunteers shall dress appropriately for the conditions and performance of their duties.

2.8 Timesheets

Individual volunteers are responsible for the accurate completion and timely submission of timesheets.

3. Volunteer recruitment and selection

3.1 Job descriptions

Volunteer staff, just as paid staff, require a clear, complete, and current description of the duties and responsibilities of the job which they are expected to fill. Prior to any volunteer assignment or recruitment effort, a job description must be developed for each volunteer post. This will be given to each accepted volunteer and used in subsequent management and evaluation efforts. Job descriptions should be reviewed and updated at least every two years, or whenever the work involved in the position changes substantially.

All job descriptions shall include a description of the purpose and duties of the job, a designated supervisor and worksite, a timeframe for the performance of the job, a listing of job qualifications, and a description of job benefits. The volunteer management department is available to assist staff in the development of volunteer jobs and job descriptions.

3.2 Staff requests for volunteers

Requests for volunteers shall be submitted in writing by interested staff, complete with a draft position description and a requested timeframe. All parties should understand that the recruitment of volunteers is enhanced by creative and interesting jobs and by advance notice. The volunteer management department reserves the right to refuse to recruit or place any volunteers until staff are prepared to make effective use of the volunteer resource.

3.3 Recruitment

Volunteers shall be recruited by the organisation on a pro-active basis, with the intent of broadening and expanding the volunteer involvement of the community. Volunteers shall be recruited without regard to gender, handicap, age, race or other condition. The sole qualification for volunteer recruitment shall be suitability to perform a task on behalf of the organisation. Volunteers may be recruited either through an interest in specific functions or through a general interest in volunteering which will later be matched with a specific function. No final acceptance of a volunteer shall take place without a specific written volunteer job description for that volunteer.

3.4 Recruitment of minors

Volunteers who have not reached the age of majority must have the written consent of a parent or guardian prior to volunteering. The volunteer services assigned to a minor should be performed in a non-hazardous environment and should comply with all appropriate requirements of child labour laws.

3.5 Interviewing

Prior to being assigned or appointed to a position, all volunteers will be interviewed to ascertain their suitability for and interest in that position. The interview should determine the qualifications of the volunteer, their commitment to fulfil the requirements of the position, and should answer any questions that the volunteer might have about the job. Interviews may be conducted either in person or by other means.

3.6 Health screening

In cases where volunteers will be working with clients with health difficulties, a health screening procedure may be required prior to confirming the volunteer assignment. In addition, if there are physical requirements necessary for performance of a volunteer task, a screening or testing procedure may be required to ascertain the ability of the volunteer to safely perform that task.

3.7 Criminal records check

As appropriate for the protection of clients, volunteers in certain assignments may be asked to submit to a criminal record check. Volunteers who do not agree to the background check may be refused the assignment.

3.8 Placement with at-risk clients

Where volunteers are to be placed in direct contact with at-risk clients, additional screening procedures may be instituted. These procedures may include reference checks, direct background investigation, criminal record investigation and so on. Volunteers who refuse permission for conduct of these checks will not be accepted for placement with clients.

3.9 Certificate of ability

Any potential volunteer who indicates that they are under the care of a doctor for either physical or psychological treatment may be asked to present a certificate from the doctor as to their ability to satisfactorily and safely perform their volunteer duties. Volunteers under a course of treatment which might affect their volunteer work will not be accepted without written verification of suitability from their doctor. Any volunteer who, after acceptance and assignment by the organisation, enters a course of treatment which might adversely impact upon the performance of their volunteer duties should consult with the volunteer programme manager.

3.10 Placement

In placing a volunteer in a position, attention shall be paid to the interests and capabilities of the volunteer and to the requirements of the volunteer position. No placement shall be made unless the requirements of both the volunteer and the supervising staff can be met: no volunteer should be assigned to a 'make-work' position and no position should be given to an unqualified or uninterested volunteer.

3.11 Staff participation in interviewing and placement

Wherever possible, staff who will be working with the volunteer should participate in the design and conduct of the interview. Final assignment of a potential volunteer should not take place without the approval of appropriate staff with whom the volunteer will be working.

3.12 Acceptance and appointment

Service as a volunteer with the organisation shall begin with an official notice of acceptance or appointment to a volunteer position. Notice may only be given by an authorised representative of the organisation, who will normally be the volunteer programme manager. No volunteer shall begin performance of any position until they have been officially accepted for that position and have completed all necessary screening and paperwork. At the time of final acceptance, each volunteer shall complete all necessary enrolment paperwork and shall receive a copy of their job description and agreement of service with the organisation.

3.13 Probationary period

All volunteer placements shall initially be done on a trial period of 30 days. At the end of this period a second interview with the volunteer shall be conducted, at which point either the volunteer or staff may request a re-assignment of the volunteer to a different position or may determine the unsuitability of the volunteer for a position within the organisation.

3.14 Re-assignment

Volunteers who are at any time re-assigned to a new position shall be interviewed for that position and shall receive all appropriate orientation and training for that position before they begin work. In addition, any screening procedures appropriate for that specific position must be completed, even if the volunteer has already been working with the organisation.

3.15 Professional services

Volunteers shall not perform professional services for which certification or a licence is required unless currently certified or licensed to do so. A copy of such certificate or licence should be maintained by the volunteer management department.

3.16 Length of service

All volunteer positions shall have a set term of duration. It is highly recommended that this term shall not be longer than one year, with an option for renewal at the discretion of both parties. All volunteer assignments shall end at the conclusion of their set term, without expectation or requirement of re-assignment of that position to the incumbent.

Volunteers are neither expected nor required to continue their involvement with the organisation at the end of their set term, although in most cases they are welcome to do so. They may instead seek a different volunteer assignment within the organisation or with another organisation, or may retire from volunteer service.

3.17 Leave of absence

At the discretion of the supervisor, leaves of absence may be granted to volunteers. This leave of absence will not alter or extend the previously agreed upon ending date of the volunteer's term of service.

4. Volunteer training development

4.1 Orientation

All volunteers will receive a general orientation on the nature and purpose of the organisation, an orientation on the nature and operation of the programme or activity for which they are recruited, and a specific orientation on the purposes and requirements of the position which they are accepting.

4.2 On-the-job training

Volunteers will receive specific on-the-job training to provide them with the information and skills necessary to perform their volunteer assignment. The timing and methods for delivery of such training should be appropriate to the complexity and demands of the position and the capabilities of the volunteer.

4.3 Staff involvement in orientation and training

Staff members with responsibility for delivery of services should have an active role in the design and delivery of both orientation and training of volunteers. Staff who will be in a supervisory capacity to volunteers shall have primary responsibility for design and delivery of on-the-job training to those volunteers assigned to them.

4.4 Volunteer involvement in orientation and training

Experienced volunteers should be included in the design and delivery of volunteer orientation and training.

4.5 Continuing education

Just as with staff, volunteers should attempt to improve their levels of skill during their terms of service. Additional training and educational opportunities will be made available to volunteers during their connection with the organisation where deemed appropriate. This continuing education may include both additional information on performance of their current volunteer assignment as well as more general information, and might be provided either by the organisation or by assisting the volunteer to participate in educational programmes provided by other groups.

4.6 Conference attendance

Volunteers are authorised to attend conferences and meetings which are relevant to their volunteer assignments, including those run by the organisation and those run by other organisations. Prior approval from the volunteer's supervisor should be obtained before attending any conference or meeting if attendance will interfere with the volunteer's work schedule or if reimbursement of expenses is sought.

5. Volunteer supervision and evaluation

5.1 Requirement of a supervisor

Each volunteer who is accepted to a position with the organisation must have a clearly identified supervisor who is responsible for direct management of that volunteer. This supervisor shall be responsible for day-to-day management and guidance of the work of the volunteer, and shall be available to the volunteer for consultation and assistance.

5.2 Volunteers as volunteer supervisors

A volunteer may act as a supervisor of other volunteers, provided that the supervising volunteer is under the direct supervision of a paid member of staff.

5.3 Volunteer-staff relationships

Volunteers and staff are considered to be partners in implementing the mission and programmes of the organisation, with each having an equal but complementary role to play. It is essential for the proper operation of this relationship that each partner understand and respect the needs and abilities of the other.

5.4 Acceptance of volunteers by staff

Since individual staff are in a better position to determine the requirements of their work and their own abilities, no volunteer will be assigned to work with a member of staff without the consent of that person. Since volunteers are considered a valuable resource in performing the organisation's work, staff are encouraged to consider creative ways in which volunteers might be of service to the organisation and to consult with the volunteer management department if they feel in need of assistance or additional training.

5.5 Volunteer management training for members of staff

An orientation on working with volunteers will be provided to all staff. In-service training on effective volunteer deployment and use will be provided to those staff who are highly involved in volunteer management.

5.6 Volunteer involvement in staff evaluation

Examination of their effective use of volunteers may be a component in the evaluation of staff performance where that member of staff is working with volunteers. In such cases, supervisors should ask for the input and participation of those volunteers in evaluating staff performance.

5.7 Staff involvement in volunteer evaluation
Affected staff should be involved in all evaluation and in deciding all work assignments of volunteers with whom they are working.

5.8 Lines of communication
Volunteers are entitled to all necessary information pertinent to the performance of their work assignments. Accordingly, volunteers should be included in and have access to all appropriate information, memos, materials, and meetings relevant to the work assignments. To facilitate the receipt of this information on a timely basis, volunteers should be included on all relevant distribution schedules and should be given a tray for receipt of information circulated in their absence. Primary responsibility for ensuring that the volunteer receives such information will rest with the direct supervisor of the volunteer.

Lines of communication should operate in both directions, and should exist both formally and informally. Volunteers should be consulted regarding all decisions which would substantially affect the performance of their duties.

5.9 Absenteeism
Volunteers are expected to perform their duties on a regular scheduled and punctual basis. When expecting to be absent from a scheduled duty, volunteers should inform their staff supervisor as far in advance as possible so that alternative arrangements may be made. Continual absenteeism will result in a review of the volunteer's work assignment or term of service.

5.10 Substitution
Volunteers may be encouraged to find a substitute for any future absences which could be filled by another volunteer. Such substitution should only be taken following consultation with a supervisor, and care should be taken to find a substitute who is qualified for the position. Substitutes may only be recruited from those who are currently enrolled as volunteers with the organisation.

5.11 Standards of performance
Standards of performance shall be established for each volunteer position. These standards should list the work to be done in that position, measurable indicators of whether the work was accomplished to the required standards, and appropriate timeframes for accomplishment of the work. Creation of these standards will be a joint function of staff and the volunteer assigned to the position, and a copy of the standards should be provided to the volunteer along with a copy of their job description at the beginning of their assignment.

5.12 Evaluation

Volunteers shall receive periodic evaluation to review their work. The evaluation session will review the performance of the volunteer, suggest any changes in work style, seek suggestions from the volunteer on means of enhancing the volunteer's relationship with the organisation, convey appreciation to the volunteer, and ascertain the continued interest of the volunteer in serving in that position. Evaluations should include both an examination of the volunteer's performance of his or her responsibilities and a discussion of any suggestions that the volunteer may have concerning the position or project with which the volunteer is connected.

The evaluation session is an opportunity for both the volunteer and the organisation to examine and improve their relationship.

5.13 Written basis for evaluation

The job description and standards of performance for a volunteer position should form the basis of an evaluation. A written record should be kept of each evaluation session.

5.14 Staff responsibility for evaluation

It shall be the responsibility of each member of staff in a supervisory relationship with a volunteer to schedule and perform periodic evaluation and to maintain records of the evaluation.

5.15 Corrective action

In appropriate situations, corrective action may be taken following an evaluation. Examples of corrective action include the requirement for additional training, re-assignment of the volunteer to a new position, suspension of the volunteer, or dismissal from volunteer service.

5.16 Dismissal of a volunteer

Volunteers who do not adhere to the rules and procedures of the organisation or who fail satisfactorily to perform their volunteer assignment may be subject to dismissal. No volunteer will be terminated until the volunteer has had an opportunity to discuss the reasons for possible dismissal with supervisory staff. Prior to dismissal of a volunteer, any affected member of staff should seek the consultation and assistance of the volunteer programme manager.

5.17 Reasons for dismissal

Possible grounds for dismissal may include, but are not limited to, the following: gross misconduct or insubordination, being under the influence of alcohol or drugs, theft of property or misuse of organisation equipment or materials, abuse or mistreatment of clients or co-workers, failure to abide by organisation policies and procedures, failure to meet physical or mental standards of performance, and failure satisfactorily to perform assigned duties.

5.18 Concerns and grievances

Decisions involving corrective action of a volunteer may be reviewed for appropriateness. If corrective action is taken, the affected volunteer shall be informed of the procedures for expressing their concern or grievance.

5.19 Notice of departure or re-assignment of a volunteer

In the event that a volunteer departs from the organisation, whether voluntarily or involuntarily, or is re-assigned to a new position, it shall be the responsibility of the volunteer management department to inform those affected staff and clients that the volunteer is no longer assigned to work with them. In cases of dismissal for good reason, this notification should be given in writing and should clearly indicate that any further contact with the volunteer must be outside the scope of any relationship with the organisation.

5.20 Resignation

Volunteers may resign from their volunteer service with the organisation at any time. It is requested that volunteers who intend to resign provide advance notice of their departure and a reason for their decision.

5.21 Exit interviews

Exit interviews, where possible, should be conducted with volunteers who are leaving their positions. The interview should ascertain why the volunteer is leaving the position, suggestions the volunteer may have for improving the position, and the possibility of involving the volunteer in some other capacity with the organisation in the future.

5.22 Communication with the volunteer management department

Staff supervising volunteers are responsible for maintaining regular communication with the volunteer management department on the status of the volunteers they are supervising, and are responsible for the timely provision of all necessary paperwork to the department. The department should be informed immediately of any substantial change in the work or status of a volunteer and should be consulted in advance before any corrective action is taken.

5.23 Evaluation of the organisation's volunteer usage

The volunteer management department shall conduct an annual evaluation of the use of volunteers by the organisation. This evaluation will include information gathered from volunteers, staff, and clients.

6. Volunteer support and recognition

6.1 Reimbursement of expenses

Volunteers are [*may be*] eligible for reimbursement of reasonable expenses incurred while undertaking business for the organisation. The volunteer management department shall distribute information to all volunteers regarding specific reimbursable items. Prior approval must be sought for any major expenditure.

6.2 Access to organisation property and materials

As appropriate, volunteers shall have access to property of the organisation and those materials necessary to fulfil their duties, and shall receive training in the operation of any equipment. Property and materials shall be used only when directly required for the volunteer task. This policy includes [*does not include*] access to and use of organisation vehicles.

6.3 Insurance

Liability and accident insurance is [*is not*] provided for all volunteers engaged in the organisation's business. [*Volunteers are encouraged to consult with their own insurance agents regarding the extension of their personal insurance to include community volunteer work. Specific information regarding such insurance is available from the volunteer management department.*]

6.4 Recognition

An annual volunteer recognition event will be conducted to highlight and reward the contribution of volunteers to the organisation. Volunteers will be consulted and involved in order to develop an appropriate format for the event.

6.5 Informal recognition

All staff and volunteers responsible for volunteer supervision are encouraged to undertake methods of recognition of volunteer service on a regular basis throughout the year. These methods of informal recognition should range from a simple "thank you" to a concerted effort to include volunteers as full participants in decision making and implementation for projects which involve the volunteer.

6.6 Volunteer career paths

Volunteers are encouraged to develop their skills while serving with the organisation, and are to be assisted through promotion to new volunteer jobs to assume additional and greater responsibilities. If so desired by the volunteer, the organisation will assist the volunteer in maintaining appropriate records of volunteer experience that will assist the volunteer in future career opportunities, both paid and volunteer.

6.7 Staff recognition

The volunteer management department shall design a recognition programme for staff who work well with volunteers, and shall consult with volunteers to identify appropriate staff to receive such awards.

APPENDIX B

Sample forms to be used in volunteer management

A selection of forms you might use or adapt for your organisation:

- ◆ Staff assessment survey on volunteer involvement
- ◆ Staff request form for volunteer assistance
- ◆ Volunteer job description
- ◆ Volunteer enrolment form
- ◆ Volunteer interview record
- ◆ Volunteer agreement
- ◆ Volunteer assignment log
- ◆ Volunteer time sheet
- ◆ Volunteer expenses claim form
- ◆ Volunteer contributions record
- ◆ Staff assessment of volunteer use
- ◆ Volunteer assessment of the volunteer programme
- ◆ Volunteer evaluation form

○　○　○　○　○　○　○　○　○　○　○　○　○

STAFF ASSESSMENT SURVEY ON VOLUNTEER INVOLVEMENT

As part of our plan to encourage volunteer assistance, we would like you to complete the following questionnaire. This survey is designed to help us assess our readiness to use volunteers and to determine what we need to do to ensure continued delivery of high quality services to our clients. All of the information collected will be kept confidential.

Experience with Volunteers

1. Have you previously worked in an organisation which used volunteers?

   ☐ Yes　　☐ No　　☐ Don't Know

2. Have you previously supervised any volunteers?

   ☐ Yes　　☐ No　　☐ Don't Know

3. Do you do volunteer work yourself?

   ☐ Yes　　☐ No　　☐ Used to, but not any more

Assessment of Volunteer Involvement

1. What is your overall assessment of the desirability of using volunteers in our organisation at this time?

   ☐ Very desirable　　　☐ Somewhat desirable
   ☐ Uncertain　　　　　 ☐ Not desirable at this time ☐ Would never be appropriate

2. What is your overall assessment of our organisation's current ability to work with volunteers?

   ☐ Very able　　　☐ Somewhat able　　☐ Uncertain　　☐ Not able

3. Are there any areas or types of work for which you think that volunteers are particularly needed and suited?

4. Are there any areas or types of work which you think volunteers should not do?

5. What issues or concerns would you like to see addressed before we use volunteers?

6. What type of training or help would you like to receive before you are asked to work with volunteers?

7. Are there any other comments, concerns, or questions that you would like to express about the involvement of volunteers in our agency?

Please return this questionnaire to...by...................................

STAFF REQUEST FORM FOR VOLUNTEER ASSISTANCE

Date of request _____ Department _____

Staff Contact _____ Phone _____

Brief Description of Work to be Performed
Give both goal of the job and examples of activities to be performed:

_____

_____

_____

Qualifications Sought
Include both skills and attributes needed to perform the work, and any items that might disqualify an applicant:

_____

_____

WORKSITE: _____

TIMEFRAME: _____

HOURS PREFERRED:

☐ Flexible to availability of volunteer   ☐ Required:_____

LENGTH OF COMMITMENT SOUGHT:

☐ Open-ended   ☐ Minimum of: _____
☐ Fixed period: _____

When do you want this job to start?

☐ Upon availability   ☐ Start date: _____

NUMBER OF VOLUNTEERS SOUGHT FOR THIS POSITION:
Please return this form to:
Name: _____
Address: _____

_____

We will be happy to work with you in completing this form. Call us at ....
if you would like assistance in developing new volunteer jobs or in learning more about
working effectively with volunteers.

VOLUNTEER JOB DESCRIPTION

Title/Position: _____

Goal of Position: _____

Sample Activities:

    1. _____

    2. _____

    3. _____

    4. _____

Timeframe:

Length of commitment: _____

Estimated total hours: _____

    Scheduling:

    ☐ At discretion of volunteer

    ☐ Required: _____

Worksite: _____

Qualifications sought:

    1. _____

    2. _____

    3. _____

    4. _____

Benefits to the volunteer:

    1. _____

    2. _____

For further information:

    Contact: _____

    Phone: _____ Date: _____

VOLUNTEER ENROLLMENT FORM

Name: _____ Phone: (Home) _____ (Work) _____

Address: _____

Contact in emergency: Name: _____ Phone: _____

Skills and interests:

Educational Background: _____

Current Occupation: _____

Hobbies, Interests, Skills: _____

Previous Volunteer Experience: _____

IS THERE A PARTICULAR TYPE OF VOLUNTEER WORK IN WHICH YOU ARE INTERESTED? *(Tick all that apply)*

☐ No preference   ☐ Working one-on-one with a single client

☐ Working directly with a member of staff as an assistant   ☐ Providing a service to several clients

☐ Helping in general administration duties   ☐ Public Speaking

☐ Fundraising   ☐ Editing a newsletter

☐ Doing research, teaching, or an individual project   ☐ Other: _____

IS THERE A CLIENT OR GROUP WITH WHOM YOU ARE PARTICULARLY INTERESTED IN WORKING?

☐ Adults   ☐ Elderly   ☐ Teens   ☐ Children

☐ Handicapped   ☐ Males   ☐ Females   ☐ No Preference

☐ Other: ☐ Not interested in working with clients

ARE THERE ANY GROUPS YOU WOULD NOT FEEL COMFORTABLE WORKING WITH?

☐ No ☐ Yes _____

Availability

AT WHAT TIMES ARE YOU INTERESTED IN VOLUNTEERING?

☐ Flexible   ☐ Prefer weekdays   ☐ Prefer weekends   ☐ Prefer daytime ☐ Prefer evenings

☐ Other: ☐ There are times during the week that I cannot do volunteer work: _____

Do you have a geographic preference as to where you do volunteer work: ☐ No ☐ Yes: _____

Do you have access to a car you can use for volunteer work?   ☐ Yes ☐ No ☐ Occasionally

References

HOW DID YOU HEAR ABOUT US?

☐ Advertisement   ☐ From client of the organisation   ☐ Referred by a volunteer

☐ Referred by a friend   ☐ Other: _____   ☐ Volunteer Bureau

NAME AND PHONE NUMBERS OF TWO PERSONAL REFEREES:

Name: _____ Phone: _____

Name: _____ Phone: _____

Please return this form to: _____

VOLUNTEER INTERVIEW RECORD

Interviewer: _____ Date: _____

Name of Volunteer: _____ Phone: _____

Review of Enrolment Form

Clarify information on Volunteer Enrolment Form. Correct information supplied on the form and place other comments below.

Non-Directive Questions

1. What attracted you to our organisation? Is there any aspect of our work that most motivates you to volunteer here?

   _____

2. What would you like to get out of volunteering here? What would make you feel like you've been successful?

   _____

3. What have you enjoyed most about your previous volunteer work?

   _____

4. What have you previously enjoyed about your paid job?

   _____

5. How would you like to be supervised?

   _____

6. Would you rather work on your own, with a group, or with a partner? Why?

   _____

7. What skills do you feel you have to contribute?

   _____

8. What can I tell you about our organisation?

   _____

Match with Volunteer Positions

Discuss potential positions and check match of interests, qualifications, and availability.

Position   Comments

1. _____   _____

2. _____   _____

3. _____   _____

VOLUNTEER INTERVIEW RECORD (CONT)

To be completed after interview.

Interviewee Assessment

APPEARANCE:

☐ Poised, neat   ☐ Acceptable   ☐ Unkempt

HEALTH AND PHYSICAL ABILITY: _____

REACTIONS TO QUESTIONS:

☐ Helpful, interested, volunteers information   ☐ Answers questions
☐ Evasive   ☐ Confused

DISPOSITION:

☐ Outgoing, confident   ☐ Reserved   ☐ Pleasant
☐ Withdrawn, moody   ☐ Suspicious, antagonistic ☐ Nothing remarkable

INTERPERSONAL SKILLS:

☐ Adept at dealing with others   ☐ Relatively at ease with others   ☐ Uncomfortable

Recommended Action

☐ Consider for following positions:

1. _____
2. _____

☐ Schedule for second interview.

☐ Hold in reserve for position of:

1. _____
2. _____

☐ Investigate further: _____

☐ Refer to: _____

☐ Not suitable for organisation at this time

Notification

☐ Volunteer notified of decision:

Name: _____

Date and method of contact: _____

VOLUNTEER AGREEMENT

This agreement is intended to indicate the seriousness with which we treat our volunteers. The intention of the agreement is to assure you both of our deep appreciation of your services and to indicate our commitment to do the very best we can to make your volunteer experience here a productive and rewarding one.

The Organisation

We, _____ (the organisation), agree to accept the

services of _____ (volunteer)

beginning _____ , and commit to the following:

1. To provide adequate information, training, and assistance for the volunteer to be able to meet the responsibilities of their volunteer job.

2. To ensure satisfactory supervisory support to the volunteer and to provide feedback on performance.

3. To respect the skills, dignity and individual needs of the volunteer, and to do our best to adjust to these individual requirements.

4. To be receptive to any comment from the volunteer regarding ways in which we might mutually better accomplish our respective tasks.

5. To treat the volunteer as an equal partner with the organisation's staff, jointly responsible for completion of the organisation's goals and the fulfilment of its mission.

The Volunteer

Agrees to serve as a volunteer and commits to the following:

1. To perform my volunteeer duties to the best of my ability.

2. To adhere to the organisation's rules and procedures, including record-keeping requirements and confidentiality of organisation and client information.

3. To meet time and duty commitments, except in exceptional circumstances, or to provide adequate notice so that alternative arrangements can be made.

Agreed to:

_____

Date _____ Date _____

This agreement may be cancelled at any time at the discretion of either of the parties, but will expire automatically on _____ unless renewed by both parties.

VOLUNTEER ASSIGNMENT LOG

Position (or department): _____ Month: _____

This is a multiple use form for tracking volunteer assignments. If labelled by 'Month' in the upper right hand corner, the form becomes a month-by-month master list of all volunteers. If labelled 'Position', the sheet records all volunteers working in a particular job. If labelled 'Department', the form records all volunteers assigned to that department.

NAME	DEPARTMENT	POSITION	STARTING DATE	ENDING DATE	NOTES
1.					
2.					
3.					
4.					
5.					
6.					
7.					
8.					
9.					
10.					
11.					
12.					
13.					
14.					
15.					
16.					
17.					
18.					
19.					
20.					
21.					
22.					
23.					
24.					

VOLUNTEER TIME SHEET

VOLUNTEER: _____   MONTH: _____

DAY	DEPARTMENT/LOCATION	JOB ASSIGNMENT	TOTAL HOURS
1.			
2.			
3.			
4.			
5.			
6.			
7.			
8.			
9.			
10.			
11.			
12.			
13.			
14.			
15.			
16.			
17.			
18.			
19.			
20.			
21.			
22.			
23.			
24.			
		TOTAL HOURS	

Please return this form by the 7th of the next month to:

_____

VOLUNTEER EXPENSES CLAIM FORM

This form is to be used to record those expenses you incur while volunteering for us for which you wish to be reimbursed. The type of expenses for which we provide reimbursement are:

1. _____
2. _____
3. _____
4. _____

Month: _____

DATE	TYPE OF EXPENDITURE	AMOUNT
	TOTAL	

These represent an accurate account of my expenses.

Approved for reimbursement.

_____

NAME OF VOLUNTEER

SUPERVISOR

_____

DATE
Cash/Payment received

DATE

_____

VOLUNTEER SIGNATURE

PAYMENT ISSUED
For office use only

Please return this by the 7th of the next month to:

_____

VOLUNTEER CONTRIBUTIONS RECORD

This form is to be used to record donations of money, in-kind contributions, and expenses incurred while volunteering for which you are asking not to be reimbursed.

Please complete the form and submit it to .... so that we can use the information in our volunteering statistics to demonstrate the added value that our volunteers bring to the organisation. We promise confidentiality.

DATE	NATURE OF CONTRUBUTION	AMOUNT
		TOTAL

I certify that these represent an accurate portrayal of my contributions:

VOLUNTEER

SIGNATURE

DATE

STAFF ASSESSMENT OF VOLUNTEER USE

This form is to allow you to provide feedback regarding our organisation's use of volunteers.
All responses will be kept confidential.

1. Are volunteers involved in your area of direct responsibility or in your department?
   ☐ Yes ☐ No ☐ Don't Know

2. In your experience, are our volunteers adequately qualifies for the work we ask them to do?
   ☐ Yes ☐ No ☐ Don't Know

3. How would you describe the use of volunteers by our staff?
   ☐ Well used ☐ Generally well used, but some exceptions
   ☐ Generally not well used ☐ Don't know

4. Are our volunteers adequately trained for their responsibilities?
   ☐ Yes ☐ No ☐ Don't Know

5. Do you think our staff have been adequately trained in how to work with volunteers?
   ☐ Yes ☐ No ☐ Don't Know

6. What else should be done to help our staff work better with volunteers?

7. How would you describe the reaction of our clients to our volunteers?
   ☐ Favourable ☐ Mixed ☐ Unfavourable ☐ Don't Know

8. What benefits do you think we have gained by using volunteers?

   _____

9. What problems have we created throught the use of volunteers?

   _____

10. How has your own workload changed as a result of our using volunteers?
    ☐ Lessened ☐ Remained the same ☐ Increased
    ☐ Changed in type of work done

11. How would you describe the assistance you have received from the Volunteer Manager?
    ☐ Helpful ☐ Not Helpful ☐ Don't Know

12. Use the space below to make any further comments regrding our use of volunteers, any additions you would like to make to your answers to the above questions, or any suggestions you have about how we might make better use of volunteers.

    _____

    _____

Please return this questionnaire to: _____ by: _____

VOLUNTEER ASSESSMENT OF THE VOLUNTEER PROGRAMME

As part of our continued effort to improve our volunteer programme, we would like your responses to the following questions. All responses will be kept completely confidential. Do not sign the survey unless you wish to.

1. How long have you been volunteering with us?...

2. What is the best experience you have had while volunteering with us?
   ....

   What is the worst experience?
   ....

3. To what extent do you think our volunteers are accepted by the staff?
   ☐ Well accepted   ☐ Generally well respected, but some exceptions
   ☐ Mixed reception   ☐ Generally not well accepted, but some exceptions ☐ Not well accepted

4. To what extent do you think volunteers are involved in reaching decisions that affect their volunteer work?
   ☐ Well involved   ☐ Sometimes involved   ☐ Not well involved

5. To what extent do you think volunteers are accepted by clients?
   ☐ Well accepted   ☐ Mixed reception   ☐ Not well accepted

6. To what extent do you think volunteers feel comfortable with the tasks they are given?
   ☐ Comfortable   ☐ Not very comfortable   ☐ Don't know

7. Do you feel that volunteers receive sufficient induction to the organisation and its work when they start?
   ☐ Yes   ☐ No   ☐ Don't know

8. Do you feel that volunteers receive enough training in how to carry out their assignments?
   ☐ Yes   ☐ No   ☐ Don't know

9. In your experience, does your volunteer job match the description of work given to you when you were interviewed?
   ☐ Yes   ☐ Mostly   ☐ No

10. Do you find your volunteer work interesting, challenging, and rewarding?
    ☐ Yes   ☐ Mostly   ☐ No

If you answered 'No', do you have any comments on why that is?

11. Do you think that volunteers are provided with sufficient feedback by those they work with?
    ☐ Yes   ☐ More or less   ☐ No   ☐ Don't know

12. Do you think volunteers are given sufficient opportunity for increased responsibility in this organisation?
    ☐ Yes   ☐ No   ☐ Don't know

13. Can you think of any new areas with which volunteers might be of help in our organisation?

14. Can you suggest any ways that we might recruit new volunteers?

15. Overall, how would you rate our volunteeer programme? (Please circle. 1 = Terrible, 7 = Great)

    1   2   3   4   5   6   7

16. Use the space below to make any other comments regarding our organisation's use of volunteers, or any additions you would like to make to your answers to the above questions:

Please return this questionnaire to: .... by:...

VOLUNTEER EVALUATION FORM

NAME OF VOLUNTEER: _____ PERIOD COVERED : _____

POSITION: _____ DATE OF EVALUATION: _____

Position Goals

	NOT MET		SATISFACTORY		WELL MET
1. _____	1	2	3	4	5
2. _____	1	2	3	4	5
3. _____	1	2	3	4	5
4. _____	1	2	3	4	5
5. _____	1	2	3	4	5

Work Relationships

	POOR		SATISFACTORY		EXCELLENT
1. Relations with other volunteers _____	1	2	3	4	5
2. Relations with staff _____	1	2	3	4	5
3. Relations with clients _____	1	2	3	4	5
4. Meeting commitments on hours and deadlines _____	1	2	3	4	5
5. Initiative _____	1	2	3	4	5
6. Flexibility _____	1	2	3	4	5

Comments by supervisor regarding above areas:

_____

_____

Overall, how does the volunteer feel about remaining in this position?

_____

_____

What else can be done to support the volunteer in this position or to move the volunteer to a new position?

_____

_____

Signed: _____   _____

SUPERVISOR   VOLUNTEER (OPTIONAL)

_____   _____

DATE   DATE

Scheduled date of the next evaluation.

EXIT INTERVIEW QUESTIONNAIRE

We are always striving to improve the performance of our volunteer management system. As one of our volunteers, we would appreciate your help in identifying areas where we might do better. Please be as complete and honest as you can in answering these questions — all of the information collected will be kept strictly confidential, but it will help to ensure that others who volunteer receive the best possible treatment.

How long did you volunteer with us? _____

Types of volunteer positions held:

1. _____

2. _____

3. _____

4. _____

Why are you leaving? (Tick all that apply)

Job accomplished ☐   Moving House ☐   Need a change ☐

Didn't like the post I was given ☐   Didn't feel well used ☐   New paid job ☐

Can no longer meet time commitments ☐

Other: _____

What did you like best about volunteering with us?

_____

_____

What suggestions would you make for changes or improvements in our use of volunteers?

_____

_____

Overall, how would you rate your experience in volunteering with us?

TERRIBLE		AVERAGE			GREAT	
1	2	3	4	5	6	7

Please return this form to:

Name: _____

Address: _____

_____

Further Reading

The following related titles are available from the Directory of Social Change, 24 Stephenson Way, London, NW1 2DP Tel: 0171 209 5151 Fax: 0171 209 5049. (Prices exclude £2.50 p&p.)

MANAGING PEOPLE, Gill Taylor & Christine Thornton, £9.95

MANAGING RECRUITMENT & SELECTION, Gill Taylor, £10.95

VOLUNTARY MATTERS - a Guide to Management and Good Practice in the Voluntary Sector, published in association with The Media Trust, £16.95

THE VOLUNTARY SECTOR LEGAL HANDBOOK, Sandy Adirondack & James Sinclair Taylor, voluntary organisations £35.00, others £50.00

A PRACTICAL GUIDE TO PAYE FOR CHARITIES, Kate Sayer, published in association with Sayer Vincent Chartered Accountants, £9.95

The following titles are available from the National Centre for Volunteering (formerly The Volunteer Centre UK), Carriage Row, 183 Eversholt Street, London, NW1 1BU Tel: 0171 388 9888 Fax: 0171 383 0448

THE 1997 NATIONAL SURVEY OF VOLUNTARY ACTIVITY IN THE UK. Available in 1998 (price not confirmed).

VOLUNTEERING MAGAZINE, £25.00 for ten issues.

WORKING WITH VOLUNTEERS:
PERSONNEL ISSUES, Claire Thornley, £4.50
RECRUITMENT & SELECTION, David Smith, £4.50
SUPPORT, Lisa Conway, £4.50
TRAINING, Lisa Conway, £4.50

THE (HELP) I-DON'T-HAVE-ENOUGH-TIME GUIDE TO VOLUNTEER MANAGEMENT, Katherine Campbell & Susan Ellis, £11.95

THE VOLUNTEER RECRUITMENT BOOK, Susan Ellis, £15.50

FROM THE TOP DOWN, Susan Ellis, £15.50
THE ROUTE TO OPPORTUNITY SERIES:

VOLUNTEERING BY YOUNG PEOPLE, F. Niyazi & A. Dingle
VOLUNTEERING BY PEOPLE WITH DISABILITIES, F. Niyazi & A. Dingle
VOLUNTEERING BY UNEMPLOYED PEOPLE, F. Niyazi & A. Dingle
VOLUNTEERING BY BLACK PEOPLE, F. Niyazi & A. Dingle
VOLUNTEERING BY OLDER PEOPLE, F. Niyazi & A. Dingle
£5.00 each, special offer, all five for £20.00

Other titles available from the Directory of Social Change:

A GUIDE TO THE MAJOR TRUSTS VOL. 1 1997/98
Luke Fitzherbert, Susan Forester, Julio Grau, £18.95

A GUIDE TO THE MAJOR TRUSTS VOL. 2 1997/98
Paul Brown & John Smyth, £18.95

THE CD-ROM TRUSTS GUIDE
(contains information from the above Major Trusts Guides and
our four Local Trusts Guides), software developed by Funderfinder,
single CD-ROM £85.00 plus VAT = £99.88

THE GUIDE TO UK COMPANY GIVING 1998
(available Spring 1998), Paul Brown & John Smyth, £25.00

THE COMPLETE FUNDRAISING HANDBOOK
Sam Clarke & Michael Norton, published in association with ICFM, £14.95

Useful Addresses

ACTION: EMPLOYEES IN THE COMMUNITY
44 Baker Street, London, W1M 1DH Tel: 0171 224 1600

BUSINESS IN THE COMMUNITY (BITC)
44 Baker Street, London, W1M 1DH Tel: 0171 224 1600

COMMUNITY SERVICE VOLUNTEERS (CSV)
237 Pentonville Road, London, N1 9NJ Tel: 0171 278 6601

COMMUNITY DEVELOPMENT FOUNDATION (CDF)
60 Highbury Grove, London, N5 2AG Tel: 0171 226 5375

DIRECTORY OF SOCIAL CHANGE (DSC)
24 Stephenson Way, London, NW1 2DP Tel: 0171 209 5151

NATIONAL ASSOCIATION OF VOLUNTEER BUREAX (NAVB)
New Oxford House, 16 Waterloo Street, Birmingham, B2 5UG
Tel: 0121 633 4555

NATIONAL ASSOCIATION OF COUNCILS FOR VOLUNTARY SERVICE
(NACVS)
3rd Floor, Arundel Court, 177 Arundel Street, Sheffield, S1 2NU
Tel: 0114 278 6636

NATIONAL CENTRE FOR VOLUNTEERING
Carriage Row, 183 Eversholt Street, London, NW1 1BU Tel: 0171 388 9888

NATIONAL COUNCIL FOR VOLUNTARY ORGANISATIONS (NCVO)
Regents Wharf, 8 All Saints Street, London, N1 9RL Tel: 0171 713 6161

NATIONAL YOUTH AGENCY
17-23 Albion Street, Leicester, LE1 6GD Tel: 0116 285 6787

NORTHERN IRELAND COUNCIL OF VOLUNTRY ACTION
127 Ormeau Road, Belfast, BT1 4EH Tel: 01232 321 224

NORTHERN IRELAND VOLUNTEER DEVELOPMENT AGENCY
Annsgate House, 70-74 Anns Street, Belfast, BT1 4EH Tel; 01232 236 100

SCOTTISH COUNCIL FOR VOLUNTARY ORGANISATIONS
18-19 Claremont Dtreet, Edinburgh, EH7 4QD Tel: 0131 556 3882

WALES COUNCIL FOR VOLUNTARY ACTION
Llys Ifor, Crescent Road, Caerphilly, Mid Glamorgan, CF8 1XL Tel: 01222 869 224

VOLUNTEER DEVELOPMENT SCOTLAND
72 Murray Place, Stirling, FK8 2BX Tel: 01786 479593

